TECHNICAL REPORT

An Outcome Evaluation of the Success for Kids Program

Nicole Maestas, Sarah Gaillot

Sponsored by the Success for Kids Foundation

T0159301

RAND LABOR AND POPULATION

The research described in this report was conducted by RAND Labor and Population.

Library of Congress Cataloging-in-Publication Data is available for this publication.
ISBN 978-0-8330-5124-0

The RAND Corporation is a nonprofit institution that helps improve policy and decisionmaking through research and analysis. RAND's publications do not necessarily reflect the opinions of its research clients and sponsors.

RAND® is a registered trademark.

Published 2010 by the RAND Corporation
1776 Main Street, P.O. Box 2138, Santa Monica, CA 90407-2138
1200 South Hayes Street, Arlington, VA 22202-5050
4570 Fifth Avenue, Suite 600, Pittsburgh, PA 15213-2665
RAND URL: http://www.rand.org/
To order RAND documents or to obtain additional information, contact
Distribution Services: Telephone: (310) 451-7002;
Fax: (310) 451-6915; Email: order@rand.org

Preface

The Success for Kids (SFK) Foundation asked the RAND Corporation to conduct the first-ever quantitative-outcome evaluation of its after-school program. Private donations raised by the SFK Foundation for this specific purpose sponsored the evaluation. Toward this end, RAND developed an experimental research design, which included randomization of 19 new partner sites in southeast Florida to treatment and control groups and repeated assessments of teachers and children at pretest, posttest, and follow-up. Under RAND direction and oversight, SFK program staff managed data collection. RAND researchers analyzed the data and prepared this report, which describes the study design and implementation, reviews the related literature, and presents the results of data analysis for a large number of quantitative behavioral and attitudinal outcomes. It is hoped that this study will aid SFK in program development, continuous quality improvement, and strategic-planning efforts. In addition, this rigorous, quantitative study makes a significant contribution to the research literature on the effectiveness of after-school programs, which is currently dominated by nonrigorous studies.

RAND Labor and Population

This research was undertaken within RAND Labor and Population. RAND Labor and Population has built an international reputation for conducting objective, high-quality, empirical research to support and improve policies and organizations around the world. Its work focuses on labor markets, social-welfare policy, demographic behavior, immigration, international development, and issues related to aging and retirement with a common aim of understanding how policy and social and economic forces affect individual decisionmaking and the well-being of children, adults, and families.

For more information about this study, contact Nicole Maestas, economist, RAND Corporation, 1776 Main Street, P.O. Box 2138, Santa Monica, CA 90407-2138, 310-393-0411, x6705, Nicole_Maestas@rand.org. For more information about RAND Labor and Population, contact Arie Kapteyn, director, RAND Labor and Population, RAND Corporation, 1776 Main Street, P.O. Box 2138, Santa Monica, CA 90407-2138, 310-393-0411, x7973, Arie_Kapteyn@rand.org. More information about RAND Labor and Population is available on its Web site (http://www.rand.org/labor/); more information about the RAND Corporation is available online as well (http://www.rand.org).

Contents

Preface iii

Figures vii

Tables ix

Summary xi

Acknowledgments xiii

Abbreviations xv

CHAPTER ONE
Introduction 1

CHAPTER TWO
Program Description 3

CHAPTER THREE
What Do We Know About After-School Programs? 7

CHAPTER FOUR
Evaluation Design and Implementation 11
Research Design 11
Assessment Instrument: The Behavior Assessment System for Children, Second Edition 16
Data Collection 17
Randomization 18
Attrition 22
Program Dosage 28

CHAPTER FIVE
Data Quality 31
Reliability 31
Validity 33

CHAPTER SIX
Outcome Analysis 37
Teacher-Reported Data 38
Child Self-Report Data 42
Reconciling Results Across Multiple Informants 45

CHAPTER SEVEN
Conclusions and Recommendations 47

APPENDIX
Training of Teachers and Facilitators 49

References 51

Figures

4.1. SFK Evaluation Research Design 12

4.2. Map of Participating After-School–Program Sites in Miami-Dade Area, Florida 16

4.3. Attendance, by Class Number 29

Tables

2.1. Summary of Lessons in SFK Level 1: "The Game of Life" Course 4
2.2. Crosswalk Between SFK Program Goals, Target Outcomes, and Curriculum Components 6
3.1. Similar Program Evaluations 9
4.1. Location, Study Enrollment, and Neighborhood Characteristics of Participating Sites 13
4.2. Logistic Regression of Treatment Assignment on Baseline Characteristics: Teacher Reports 19
4.3. Joint Significance Tests for Table 4.2 20
4.4. Logistic Regression of Treatment Assignment on Baseline Characteristics: Child Reports 20
4.5. Joint Significance Tests for Table 4.4 22
4.6. Attrition Rates 24
4.7. Logistic Regression of Treatment Assignment on Baseline Characteristics: Teacher Reports, Nonattritors Only 24
4.8. Joint Significance Tests for Table 4.7 25
4.9. Logistic Regression of Treatment Assignment on Baseline Characteristics: Child Reports, Nonattritors Only 26
4.10. Joint Significance Tests for Table 4.9 27
4.11. Attendance, by Site 30
5.1. Data Quality: Cronbach's Alpha Reliability Coefficients 32
5.2. Data Quality: Percent of Observations with Invalid Response Patterns 34
6.1. BASC-2 Scales: Teacher (TRS-C) 39
6.2. Treatment Effects: Teacher Reports 40
6.3. BASC-2 Scales: Child (SRP-C) 43
6.4. Treatment Effects: Child Self-Reports 44

Summary

This report presents results from a multisite, quantitative evaluation of the international Success for Kids (SFK) after-school program. The program seeks to build resilience in children by teaching them to access inner resources and build positive connections with others. The level I SFK program, titled "The Game of Life," is a 10-part course offered weekly in 90-minute lessons free of charge to children between the ages of 6 and 14 who are enrolled in existing after-school programs. The course uses structured games and activities to teach such concepts as cause and effect, how to control reactive behaviors, the value of sharing with others, and the importance of making an effort. Through its curriculum, the program aims to increase prosocial behaviors and reduce antisocial and problem behaviors. The SFK program is unlike most after-school programs both in its focus on spiritual development and in its emphasis on outcomes related to resilience rather than academics.

Although after-school programs in the United States receive significant financial backing from both public and private sources, the literature assessing their effectiveness has many methodological weaknesses. Among the better studies of programs addressing social behaviors (such as SFK), program effects have been shown to be small. This study attempted to avoid the pitfalls evident in the research literature by using a very rigorous methodology: randomization of program sites to treatment and control groups and repeated measurements over time. This research design was possible owing to a unique window of opportunity: SFK was rapidly expanding its operations in southeast Florida, which enabled us to randomly assign 19 new program sites to either immediate implementation of the program or delayed implementation after a 12-week waiting period. During the waiting period, the delayed-implementation sites formed a "control group" for the sites receiving immediate implementation (the "treatment group"). The 19 program sites were diverse both in their demographic composition and in their spatial location throughout Miami-Dade, Broward, and Palm Beach counties.

Behavioral outcomes were measured using the well-known Behavior Assessment System for Children, Second Edition (BASC-2). Children and their regular after-school–program teachers (not the SFK teachers) were assessed at pretest, posttest, and follow-up. An extensive analysis of reliability and validity revealed that the self-report data collected from children were plagued with inconsistencies, and thus conclusions are based on the data collected from teachers.

We found that the program had beneficial effects on virtually every domain covered by the BASC-2. In particular, the program had medium to large effects on adaptive skills (effect sizes [ESs] of 0.55 to 0.73),[1] which include adaptability, social skills, leadership, study skills, and communication skills. The program had small to medium effects on behavioral problems (0.19 to 0.37), especially attention problems and withdrawal, and small effects on overexternalization of problems (0.16 to 0.29). The program had small to medium effects on the reported incidence of school problems (0.32 to 0.48). There is suggestive evidence that many effects persisted at 12-week follow-up. Notably, the ESs exceeded the average ESs found for after-school programs targeting similar outcomes (0.19 for positive social behaviors and 0.18 for problem behaviors), as calculated by Durlak and Weissberg (2007) in a recent meta-analysis.

Of significant interest is the finding that the program positively affected school-related outcomes, even though SFK is not an academic intervention. Specifically, the program improved reported study skills and reduced reported learning problems and attention problems. SFK's success in improving school-related outcomes suggests that an extremely interesting follow-up study would be one that examined program effects on grades and subsequent standardized test scores.

Because the program continues to expand to not only new communities but different countries and settings, we recommend a follow-up study to test the replicability of the SFK model in other contexts. For example, the program was evaluated in southeast Florida, where it is delivered in school and after-school settings, but, in other countries, notably Mexico, Panama, and Malawi, it is delivered in family centers and orphanages. Likewise, in some U.S. and Latin American sites, it is delivered in Spanish rather than English.

Also, while many program effects were reasonably persistent at 12-week follow-up, there was some variation among the outcomes in whether treatment effects rose or fell with time. This suggests that follow-up programming could be used to support the treatment effects achieved with the level 1 course. We recommend evaluation of the SFK level 2 and level 3 courses to test whether they can support and perhaps even build on the effects achieved after the level 1 course. Future evaluations might also seek to extend the follow-up period beyond 12 weeks. Overall, a major strength of the program appears to be its careful attention to uniformity of program delivery—in particular, its standardized curriculum, use of experienced teachers, and formal teacher-training program.

---

[1] ESs are calculated by dividing the estimated treatment effect by the pretest standard deviation for each scale. A positive sign is assigned to an ES whenever the treatment group did "better" than the control group, and a negative sign is used whenever the control group did "better" than the treatment group. Thus, a positive ES for a negative behavior means that the treatment group experienced a greater reduction in the behavior than did the control group.

Acknowledgments

We thank Marcelo Castro of Fischler School of Education and Human Services, Nova Southeastern University in North Miami Beach, Florida, for expert advice on numerous design and implementation issues; and Zoë Cullen and Xiaoyan Li at the Frederick S. Pardee RAND Graduate School for research assistance.

Abbreviations

BASC-2   Behavior Assessment System for Children, Second Edition

DD   difference-in-difference

ES   effect size

FCAT   Florida Comprehensive Assessment Test

i.i.d.   independent and identically distributed

PRS   parent rating scale

SFK   Success for Kids

SRP   self-report of personality

SRP-A   self-report of personality–adolescent

SRP-C   self-report of personality–child

TRS   teacher rating scale

TRS-A   teacher rating scale–adolescent

TRS-C   teacher rating scale–child

CHAPTER ONE

Introduction

Success for Kids (SFK) began working with a small number of schools in Los Angeles six years ago and has since grown rapidly to operate programs in New York, Miami, and Las Vegas, as well as internationally in London, Mexico City, Panama, Israel, and Malawi. It currently serves approximately 7,000 children worldwide. Through its 10-week level 1 course, SFK uses a non-religious, nondenominational curriculum to teach children how to access inner resources and build positive connections with others.

Despite the program's rapid expansion, fueled by growing international support, program effects have been documented only informally through testimonials. This study was the first formal evaluation of the program's quantitative effects on an array of behavioral and attitudinal outcomes. In its attention to methodological rigor, the study stands apart from the after-school–program evaluation literature, which is dominated by nonrigorous studies.

The centerpiece of the evaluation design is our use of randomized treatment and control groups formed of 737 children in 19 existing after-school programs in southeast Florida. As SFK was expanding in the region, these 19 sites were new partners that had recently agreed to offer the SFK curriculum as part of their regular after-school programming. The treatment sites received SFK programming immediately, whereas the control sites received the program after a 12-week delay. Children in both groups were surveyed at the beginning and end of the first 12-week period; however, those in the treatment group received the SFK program during the intervening weeks, whereas children in the control group did not. Accordingly, we estimate treatment effects (TEs) as pre- and postdifferences for the treatment group *relative to* pre- and postdifferences for the control group. As the design was implemented in three phases, sites that were initially control sites eventually became treatment sites, once they received programming.

Using experimental and quasiexperimental analysis methods consistent with the research design, we found that the program had beneficial effects on a large number of behavioral and attitudinal outcomes. In particular, the program had medium to large effects on adaptive skills (effect sizes [ESs] of 0.63 to 0.80), which include adaptability, social skills, leadership, study skills, and communication skills. The program had small to medium effects on the incidence of behavioral problems (0.20 to 0.34), especially attention problems and withdrawal, and it had small effects on overexternalization of problems (0.18 to 0.27) and overinternalization (0.18) of problems. The program had small to medium effects on reported school problems (0.33 to 0.48). Nearly all effects were statistically significant at the 5-percent level. Notably, the ESs exceed the average ESs found for after-school programs targeting similar outcomes (0.19 for positive social behaviors and 0.18 for problem behaviors), as calculated by Durlak and

Weissberg (2007) in their recent meta-analysis. There is suggestive evidence that many effects persisted at 12-week follow-up.

In Chapter Two, the report continues with a description of the program and its 10-week curriculum. Chapter Three provides a brief survey of the related program-evaluation literature. Chapter Four describes our research design and its implementation. In that chapter, we describe the randomization procedure, quasiexperimental adjustments for baseline differences, our assessment instrument, data collection, attrition, and program dosage. Chapter Five presents results from an analysis of data quality. Chapter Six presents estimated TEs and ESs for the many outcomes we analyzed. Finally, Chapter Seven concludes with discussion and recommendations.

CHAPTER TWO

Program Description

The mission of SFK is "to empower kids to lead happy and productive lives by providing them with a sense of purpose and the recognition that they have the power to impact the course and direction of their lives." The philosophy underlying this mission is that resilience, or the ability to overcome adverse circumstances in daily life, is a universal quality, rather than a quality that only some children possess. The program is not a religious program; rather, it teaches children to access inner resources and build positive connections with others.

The level 1 SFK course, titled "The Game of Life," consists of 10 90-minute lessons and typically runs over a 10-week period. The course is built on the analogy that, as in a game, the challenges we overcome in life bring a sense of achievement that makes us happy. Children are taught that they can "win the game" and achieve their potential when they follow the "rules"—making an effort, caring for others, and making responsible choices. Table 2.1 presents a summary of each of the 10 lessons, as well as examples of specific program activities. As the many examples illustrate, the course is experiential in nature, using teaching methods that include stories, puppets, music, performance, and hands-on activities in an attempt to address auditory, kinesthetic, and visual learning styles. All concepts taught in the curriculum are continuously reinforced within a lesson and across all subsequent lessons in the course.

The SFK curriculum is based on established best practices in the resiliency literature that seek to build four areas of personal strength: social competence, problem solving, autonomy or self-efficacy, and sense of purpose (Benard, 2004; Werner and Smith, 1992). The SFK curriculum is notable in that it attempts to build resiliency by addressing all four areas of resiliency, not only sense of purpose. Although causal studies are lacking, several studies have documented a positive correlation between youth spiritual development and aspects of resiliency, such as prosocial behaviors, as well as a negative correlations with antisocial and problem behaviors, such as suicide and drug use (see Donahue and Benson, 1995, for a review). A recent meta-analysis of "positive youth-development" programs funded by the U.S. Department of Health and Human Services listed spiritual development as one of a set of objectives for programs seeking to promote positive outcomes for youth (Catalano et al., 2004).

Consistent with the mission of building resiliency in children, the specific program goals of the SFK curriculum are

1. to increase children's sense of empowerment about their ability to influence their future
2. to provide the knowledge, attitudes, and skills needed to make positive choices
3. to increase caring and empathy

4. to improve the quality of family interaction (including communication, doing activities together, sharing, and asking permission)
5. to increase happiness.

Table 2.1
Summary of Lessons in SFK Level 1: "The Game of Life" Course

Lesson	Core Idea	Sample Activities
1: What Do We Want?	The children consider the physical things they want and how having these things makes them feel. They learn that these feelings and emotions—and not the physical things themselves—are what they really want.	The children make a list of things they want then describe how having those things would make them feel. They learn that what they really want is the feelings and emotions that the things evoke, not the things themselves. Activities with scales and measuring tapes are performed to teach that physical things can be measured, weighed, touched, or counted, whereas feelings and emotions cannot. Feelings and emotions—such as happiness, joy, love, comfort, protection, and confidence—are the spiritual power or "light" inside all things and experiences.
2: Making Choices	The children discover that we always have choices about our own actions. We can choose to care, share, and think of others, or we can choose to think only of ourselves and take the easy way out.	Through a puppet show, students learn to identify two inner voices—the "good guy," who encourages us to care, share, and think of others, and the "opponent," who tells us to think only of ourselves or take the easy way out. Students give examples of the two voices in their lives through worksheets, discussions, and art activities.
3: Making an Effort	The children learn that, when we work hard for something and put in maximum effort, we earn greater satisfaction and appreciation of our own worth.	A story is told about a puzzle maker who always dazzles students with a new and exciting puzzle each week. One week, he decides to give the puzzle to the kids already solved. Students examine how there is little satisfaction in getting something without earning it. The students think of areas in which the opponent tells them not to put in effort. They make commitment cards to help remind them to make an effort in these areas over the subsequent week.
4: Caring for Others	The children learn the value and benefit of teamwork.	Small groups of students are given spoons and one bowl of cereal. They are told that they may use their spoons to eat as much cereal as they want but they cannot bend their arms. After trying to feed themselves without bending their arms, the students realize that if they feed each other, they can all eat. Students develop a friendship scrapbook that introduces the meaning of caring for others. They fill in the scrapbook by asking each other about themselves and communicating outside of classes.
5: Feelings and Behavior	The children learn how to identify feelings that bring them down (such as sadness, anger, loneliness, and disappointment) and discover how to stop their reactive behaviors (such as fighting, bullying, shouting, and withdrawal) caused by these feelings.	Students learn that they can stop their reactive behavior by asking their good guy to guide them and by sharing. In this lesson, students think about times when they have been reactive and generate alternative solutions. Using a bowl of dirty water to represent our reactive feelings and a sponge to represent us, students learn that, when they have negative feelings, it can be very difficult to listen to the voice of the good guy. To do this, they have to stop before they act, restrict (squeeze the dirty water out of the sponge), and ask the good guy to guide us (dip in clean water). This concept is reinforced in student worksheets and discussions using practical examples from their daily lives.

Table 2.1—Continued

Lesson	Core Idea	Sample Activities
6: Sharing	The children learn that, the more we share of our time, talents, love, and possessions, the more others are likely to share with us.	Students learn that, through sharing, they actually receive more (not less) and are able to change the quality of their own lives as well as the world around them. One example is a demonstration in which students are asked to find a way in which water being poured from a jug representing all the things we want in life (e.g., happiness, love, friendship) can be continuously received by us (represented by a cup). After seeing that, once the cup is full, it can accept no more water, they realize that only by poking a hole in the bottom of the cup and letting the water flow through into another cup, can they continuously pour water from the jug into the cup. Through this activity, they learn that only by sharing with others can they make room for a continuous flow of life's blessings.
7: We Are All Connected	The children learn how they can have an impact on the well-being of others by being concerned with tolerance, human dignity, and respect.	Students learn about the light within each of us and how we are all connected. Students make beaded necklaces in an art activity. They learn that the string holding us all together (represented by the string connecting the beads) can be cut whenever we listen to the voice of the opponent and engage in reactive behavior thinking only of ourselves. Through this activity, students consider the effects of their actions on themselves and others.
8: Cause and Effect	The children discover that everything they do has consequences and thus learn to take responsibility for their own behavior.	Students are introduced to the spiritual concept that how they act (cause) determines future circumstances (effect). Students engage in a musical game in which students with positive action statements circle around an equal number of students with positive effect statements. Whenever the music stops, the students exchange cause and effect statements with the partner with whom they end up. A discussion helps the students understand that their positive actions always have later positive effects—even when the link between cause and effect does not match exactly. This activity is repeated with negative cause and effect statements.
9: Telling People You Care	The children learn to express their appreciation for others.	The children make cards to tell a loved one how they feel and how much they appreciate this special person in their lives.
10: Review and Graduation	The children review what they have learned and receive recognition.	The children receive certificates recognizing their efforts during the course.

Table 2.2 shows how these program goals map to specific target outcomes, such as increasing prosocial behaviors and decreasing problem behaviors. It also relates each of the 10 lessons to specific goals and outcomes.

The SFK curriculum is geared toward children ages 6 to 14. Program organizers have sought to target children living in lower-income communities, those challenged by poor school performance, crime, and lack of community services; however, none of these factors is a requirement for participation in the program. The program takes the view that resiliency is an innate capacity that exists in all children and that all children, regardless of race, culture, or location, can benefit from resiliency building. Notably, the SFK program is free to participating agencies and families.

The SFK curriculum is portable. It can be taught in any setting and, to date, has been taught mainly in either SFK-owned facilities or in partnership with local public schools and

Table 2.2
Crosswalk Between SFK Program Goals, Target Outcomes, and Curriculum Components

Goals	Outcomes	Curriculum Component
To increase children's sense of empowerment about their ability to affect their future	A significant reduction in behaviors indicating anxiety A significant increase in prosocial behaviors, such as asking others for information, introducing oneself, and responding appropriately to the actions of others	Lesson 2: Making Choices Lesson 8: Cause and Effect
To provide the knowledge, attitudes, and skills needed to make positive choices	A significant reduction in inappropriate behaviors, such as verbal or physical aggression, poor control of temper, arguing, and hyperactivity A significant increase in such behaviors as helping others, sharing materials, and complying with rules and directions A significant increase in self-control behaviors, such as responding appropriately to teasing and taking turns and compromising	Lesson 5: Feelings and Behavior Lesson 6: Sharing Lesson 3: Making an Effort
To increase caring and empathy	A significant increase in behaviors that show concern and respect for others' feelings and viewpoints	Lesson 4: Caring for Others Lesson 5: Feelings and Behavior Lesson 6: Sharing Lesson 7: We Are All Connected Lesson 8: Cause and Effect
To improve the quality of family interaction (including communication, doing activities together, sharing, and asking permission)	A significant increase in behaviors that demonstrate an ability to communicate with adults and regard for property or work	Lesson 3: Making an Effort
To increase self-reported happiness	A significant decrease in behaviors indicating sadness, loneliness, and poor self-esteem	Lesson 1: What Do We Want? Lesson 7: We Are All Connected

after-school programs. Regardless of setting, classes are always taught by professional SFK teachers, who have undergone a three-month, formal SFK training program. Teachers are assisted by a group of three to five facilitators, who are tasked with helping the children relate course principles to actual situations in their lives. A brief overview of the training process of SFK teachers and facilitators is included in the appendix. While classes may be delivered in either English or Spanish, all classes taught during the study were delivered in English.

CHAPTER THREE

What Do We Know About After-School Programs?

An estimated 7 million U.S. children spend some period after school with no adult supervision, putting them at risk for negative academic and behavioral outcomes. But children can benefit when they engage in structured out-of-school-time activities. How much and in what ways, however, is an open question: Most reviews of out-of-school-time programs have focused on academic benefits, show mixed results, and are not rigorous (Durlak and Weissberg, 2007). This may be because the programs themselves vary greatly in quality and participation rates. Given the large financial backing for out-of-school-time programs, stakeholders are increasingly interested in knowing whether the programs are improving outcomes and reaching those most in need (Little and Harris, 2003).

Evaluations of out-of-school-time programs link participation to greater academic involvement and motivation, higher achievement, higher attendance, and fewer disciplinary actions (Little and Harris, 2003). However, these studies are plagued with problems. For example, few evaluations use a control group. Because those who attend an out-of-school-time program may be systematically different from those who do not attend, it is difficult to conclude that differences between these groups are wholly attributable to TEs.

Another limitation is that many existing studies are "black-box" evaluations, in which it is impossible to untangle what elements make the program successful for what types of students. This makes it difficult, for example, to judge whether a different program might have similar effects with a different population or to infer causality between specific program activities and specific outcomes (Little and Harris, 2003). Studies that do analyze program features tend to rely on expert opinion (Bodilly and Beckett, 2005; Scott-Little, Hamann, and Jurs, 2002). Most include evaluations published outside of peer-reviewed journals and with numerous threats to internal validity (Bodilly and Beckett, 2005). Further, much of the research has focused on middle-class, Caucasian students, making the results difficult to generalize (Fashola, 1998). For all of these reasons, inferences from the literature must be drawn with caution.

Much of the research on out-of-school-time programs has overlooked personal and social benefits of out-of-school-time programs, and there has been little attempt to describe effective programs that target these areas. Durlak and Weissberg (2007) completed the first meta-analysis of out-of-school-time programs promoting personal and social skills. Through systematic searches, they identified 66 programs that promote personal or social skills in young people between the ages of 5 and 18, were evaluated using a comparison group and post data, presented sufficient information to calculate ESs, and appeared by the end of 2005. The programs had to operate during at least part of the school year, occur outside of normal school hours, and be supervised or monitored by adults, and they excluded programs that reported only outcomes for academic performance or school attendance, programs that focused on adventure education or were social events offered in the community, and extracurricular school activities. Sixty-seven percent of these studies were unpublished, 26 percent employed randomized designs, 69 percent reported acceptable reliability, 85 percent had no problems with attrition, and 60 percent appeared after 2000. They also looked at 14 reports that contained follow-up data but found that sample sizes were too small for any meaningful analyses.

Overall, Durlak and Weissberg found that out-of-school-time programs targeting personal and social skills significantly improve students' self-perceptions, school bonding (positive feelings and attitudes about school), positive social behaviors, achievement test scores, and school grades while reducing problem behaviors and drug use. Mean ESs for each of eight outcomes were derived by first calculating standardized mean differences by outcome category for each study and then averaging ESs by outcome category across studies. Twenty-two programs reported child self-perception outcomes, with a mean ES of 0.34, and 28 programs reported outcomes for school bonding, with a mean ES of 0.14. The mean ES for positive social behaviors was 0.19 (N=35), the mean ES for problem behaviors was 0.18 (N=42), and the mean ES for drug use was 0.11 (N=27). Finally, 20 programs reported achievement-test measures for a mean ES of 0.16, and 25 programs reported school grades for a mean ES of 0.11. All of these mean effects were significant at the 5-percent level. When the researchers compared programs that use evidence-based skill-training procedures (defined as sequential, active, focused, and explicit activities) with those that do not, only evidence-based programs (N=39) had significant mean ESs; these ranged from 0.22 for drug use to 0.35 for child self-perceptions.

We summarize several of the program evaluations reviewed by Durlak and Weissberg in Table 3.1, focusing on those programs with goals similar to SFK's and those reporting behavioral outcomes for elementary- and middle-school students. All of the evaluations included a control group, reported pre- and postquantitative differences, and are published or available online. The SFK program's goals of empowerment, making positive choices, increasing empathy and happiness, and improving family interactions are similar to the goals of the programs in Table 3.3. However, the length of the SFK program is quite short compared to the other programs listed. Like all of the studies listed, this evaluation used a control group; however, our use of randomization is notable, and the sample for this evaluation is among the larger samples in the table. Like many, we used a standardized, well-studied measurement instrument and analyzed the reliability of the measurement instrument as it pertains to our sample. Most evaluations collected data from multiple informants, as did we. A critique of our evaluation, like those presented in Table 3.3, is that it too is a black-box evaluation, in the sense that we do not identify which specific program elements contribute to various TEs. This is partly because the SFK intervention is narrow in scope as it is, but also because we did not have the resources to collect the data that would permit analyses of this nature. Finally, as we describe in Chapter Six, we found TEs across a larger number of scales than most others and, in general, larger ESs. On balance, we conclude that both our evaluation methodology and our findings compare favorably to the group of evaluations reviewed by Durlak and Weissberg (2007).

Table 3.1
Similar Program Evaluations

Program	Goal	Evaluation	N	Program Length	Measures Used	α	Results
21st-Century Community Learning Centers Program	Academic, recreational, cultural	James-Burdumy, Dynarski, and Deke (2005)	1,000	2 years	School records; original student, parent, teacher surveys	?	No effect on homework assistance, academic achievement, parental involvement; higher levels of negative behavior (e.g., more calls to parents, more suspensions) in treatment group
Austin After-School Program	Sports, art, drama, computer, cooking, cultural, math and science activities	Baker and Witt (1996)	302	6 months	Behavior Rating Profiles (adapted); Culture Free Self-Esteem Inventory-2 (selected subscales)	>0.67	Significant increase for participants in the general self-esteem scale only
Be a Star Program	Reduce drug and alcohol use by building resiliency	Pierce and Shields (1998)	783	9 months	Revised Individual Protective Factors Index; Revised Cultural Awareness Test; "Draw a Person" test	0.0–0.68	Significantly better results among treatment group for measures of family bonding, prosocial behavior, self-concept, self-control, decisionmaking, emotional awareness, assertiveness, cooperation, attitudes toward drugs and alcohol, self-efficacy, African-American culture, and school bonding
Hispanic After-School Program	Early identification and treatment of mental-health issues, promotion of ethnocultural identity	Garza Fuentes and LeCapitaine (1990)	55	4 years	Martinek-Zaichowsky Self-Concept Scale for Children; Teacher Expectancy of Academic Performance Scale; Aggression, Mood, and Learning Disabilities Scale	0.75–0.92	Treatment group had greater gains in perceived academic status, physical attributes, happiness, anxiety reduction, popularity, and better school adjustment
Kuumba Kids	Develop self-esteem and creativity, build African-based cultural awareness	Mason and Chuang (2001)	51	4 months	Behavior Assessment System for Children	0.00–0.87	Treatment group showed significantly greater gains in self-esteem, social skills, and leadership competencies

Table 3.1—Continued

Program	Goal	Evaluation	N	Program Length	Measures Used	α	Results
LA's Best	Tutoring, recreation, personal skills training, self-esteem development, nutrition	Brooks, Mojica, and Land (1995)	146	2+ years	Grades; original child and parent surveys	?	Inconclusive effect on grades; more likely to have positive attitudes and behavior, positive relationships with adults, report liking school, and have higher expectations of educational future
Maryland After-School Community Grant Program	Increase youth resiliency and prevent substance abuse, violence, and delinquency	Gottfredson et al. (2004)	825	9 months	Social Skills Rating System; "What About You" survey (adapted); original items about unsupervised after-school time and involvement in constructive activities	0.6–0.8	Participation reduced delinquent behavior only for middle-school students by increasing intentions not to use drugs and positive peer interactions
South Baltimore Youth Center	Strengthen resiliency	Belgrave et al. (2000)	147	4 months	Africentric Value Scale for Children; Children's Racial Identity Scale; Piers-Harris Self Concept Scale; Children's Sex Role Inventory	0.60–0.75	Treatment group scored significantly better on Africentric values, racial identity, and physical-appearance ratings
Study of Promising After-School Programs	19 high-quality after-school programs	Vandell, Reisner, Brown, et al. (2005); Vandell, Reisner, Pierce, et al. (2006)	1,820 in year 1; 1,434 in year 2	1 year, 2 years	Mock Report Card; Self-Efficacy; Self-reported Behavior Index; Substance Use and Risk Behaviors; Teacher Checklist of Peer Relations; Child Behavior Scale	>0.72	Significant improvements after year one for self-reports of work habits and misconduct, teacher and program staff reports of work habits, task persistence, social skills, behavior toward peers; similar results with generally larger effect sizes at end of year two
Woodrock Youth Development Project	Drug and alcohol intervention focusing on improving problem-solving skills, coping skills, and self-perception	LoSciuto, Freeman, et al. (1997); LoSciuto, Hilbert, et al. (1999)	367 in year 1, 718 in year 2	1 year, 2 years	Self-Perception Profile for Children (adapted); CSAP Knowledge, Attitude, and Behavior (adapted); original race-relations and ethnocentrism items; original measure of aggression	0.38–0.82	1-year follow-up gains in academic attendance, reductions in drug use, improvements in race relations and ethnocentrism; 2-year follow-up reductions in self-reported substance abuse, improvements in race relations, improvements in self-reported school attendance

CHAPTER FOUR

Evaluation Design and Implementation

Research Design

Our research design takes advantage of a unique window of opportunity: During late 2006, the SFK program was rapidly expanding to different existing after-school programs in southeast Florida. This dramatic growth enabled us to randomly assign the 19 participating after-school–program sites to "immediate" implementation of SFK programming and "delayed" implementation after an approximately 12-week waiting period. This is similar to using a "wait-list" control group. During the waiting period, the delayed-implementation sites formed a control group for the immediate-intervention sites.

Figure 4.1 illustrates how the design was implemented. In the fall of 2006, sites in group 1 and group 2 entered the study. Group 1 received SFK programming immediately, while programming for group 2 was delayed until the winter of 2006–2007. However, *both* groups were tested in fall 2006 and winter 2006–2007. For group 1, these were its pretest and posttest as a "treatment group"; for group 2, these were its pretest and posttest as a "control group." In winter 2006–2007, group 2 switched from control status to treatment status, and its control-group posttest simultaneously became its treatment-group pretest. Group 2's posttest as a treatment group was administered in spring 2007; at the same time, group 1 received a follow-up test. Group 3 entered the study in winter 2006–2007, first as a control group, then switching to treatment-group status in spring 2007. Its winter 2006–2007 test was its pretest as a control group, and its spring 2007 test was simultaneously its posttest as a control group and its pretest as a treatment group. Its posttest as a treatment group was administered in summer 2007, when group 2 also received its follow-up test. The study ended in summer 2007, so no follow-up data were collected for group 3.

Table 4.1 lists the names and addresses of the participating after-school–program sites, the number of children enrolled in the study at each site, and the randomization group to which the site was assigned. Characteristics of the neighborhoods surrounding each site are also shown. Clearly, the participating sites are a heterogeneous group. The local crime rate varied from a low of 4,130 per 100,000 population for the Florence A. DeGeorge Unit (Boys and Girls Club of Broward County) in the city of Davie to a high of 12,183 for Teen Upward Bound in the city of Opa Locka. Median income and the percent of single-mother households in the surrounding ZIP® code also vary dramatically across sites, as does the racial and ethnic composition of the ZIP code.[1] The dominant racial and ethnic groups in southeast

---

[1] Note that, because census racial and ethnic categories are not mutually exclusive (respondents may select more than one category), percentages do not sum to 100.

Figure 4.1
SFK Evaluation Research Design

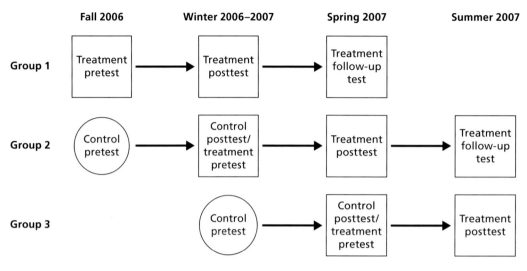

RAND *TR575-4.1*

Florida are white, black and Latino. Finally, the average academic performance of children in the surrounding community varies substantially across sites, as measured by third-grade Florida Comprehensive Assessment Test (FCAT) reading and math scores for the nearest public school. Figure 4.2 is a map showing the spatial layout of the 19 sites, which spans the counties of Miami-Dade, Broward, and Palm Beach.

Although the study was conducted in waves over the course of a year, in analyzing the data, we pooled all treatment-group observations and all control-group observations. This effectively combines the experimental variation (that induced by randomization) with quasiexperimental variation.[2] In theory, one need use only the experimental variation; this would amount to comparing group 1 with groups 2 and 3 and then group 2 with group 3. However, our preliminary analyses revealed that randomization did not sufficiently balance the covariates across treatment and control groups when defined in this way. This does not necessarily mean that randomization was implemented incorrectly; even under perfect randomization, we would expect some differences due to sampling variability among the groups, because we randomized over a small number of units (19 program sites) drawn from demographically heterogeneous neighborhoods. Such differences would tend to "average out" as the number of randomization units increased.

As noted by Cook and Campbell (1979), one strategy for remedying imperfect randomization is to reconceptualize the research design as a longitudinal study, if repeated measures are available. By letting the control sites in groups 2 and 3 also contribute treatment observations, we can pool all treatment and control observations and use site-level fixed effects, which effectively lets group 2 and 3 sites act as control groups *for themselves*. This means that children in groups 2 and 3 enter the study once as control children and again as treatment children, which naturally helps minimize observed and unobserved differences between the groups. The experimental variation is still present to a certain degree, because group 1, which never acted

---

[2] See Miguel and Kremer (2004) for another example of how experimental and quasiexperimental methods may be combined to identify TEs.

Table 4.1
Location, Study Enrollment, and Neighborhood Characteristics of Participating Sites

Site	Study Group	Children in Study	Crime Rate[a]	Single Mother (%)[b,c]	White	Black	Latino	Median Income ($)[b]	Reading	Math
					Race or Ethnicity (%)[b,d]				3rd Grade FCAT Scores[e]	
African Cultural Center; 6161 NW 22nd Ave, Miami, FL 33142	1	27	7,613	15.7	36.3	56.0	45.4	18,506	297	296
Aspira, 1 NE 19th St, Miami, FL 33132	3	72	7,613	3.2	73.6	21.7	54.1	22,969	276	280
Centro Mater East, 418 SW 4th Ave, Miami, FL 33131	2,3	40	7,613	2.1	93.3	1.7	54.6	56,297	346	376
Centro Mater West, 7700 NW 98 St, Hialeah Gardens, FL 33016	1	46	4,556	11.4	87.7	3.9	87.6	35,762	301	314
Citrus Grove Elementary (YWCA), 2121 NW 5th St, Miami, FL 33125	3	20	7,613	8.2	86.7	5.1	89.8	22,106	268	274
Concerned African Women, 16520 NW 28th Avenue, Miami, FL 33055	1	47	7,613	12.1	51.0	41.8	52.6	39,088	278	304
DeGeorge Unit (Boys and Girls Club), 1220 SW 133 Ave, Davie, FL 33325	3	37	4,130	7.5	90.6	4.5	17.4	54,682	311	330
For the Children, 1718 S. Douglas St, Lake Worth, FL 33461	2	52	10,053	9.0	78.0	10.9	29.6	32,331	308	313
Forest Park Elementary (Beacon), 1201 SW 3rd St, Boynton Beach, FL 33436	3	22	5,953	4.3	87.3	9.0	7.7	45,047	274	295

Table 4.1—Continued

Site	Study Group	Children in Study	Crime Rate[a]	Single Mother (%)[b,c]	Race or Ethnicity (%)[b,d]			Median Income ($)[b]	3rd Grade FCAT Scores[e]	
					White	Black	Latino		Reading	Math
Hialeah Elementary (YMCA), 550 E. 8th St, Hialeah, FL 33010	1	35	4,392	7.8	91.0	4.2	91.4	22,815	309	338
Lauderhill Unit (Boys and Girls Club), 5455 NW 19th St, Lauderhill, FL 33314	2	47	4,414	8.1	87.0	6.1	22.2	35,669	293	294
Milagro Center, 340 SW 6th Ave, Delray Beach, FL 33445	1	28	6,050	3.6	78.6	18.8	5.8	42,653	293	319
Nan Knox Unit (Boys and Girls Club), 832 NW 2nd St, Ft Lauderdale, FL 33312	2	45	7,423	7.9	59.2	36.3	14.9	38,190	276	281
Pleasant City, 2222 Spruce Ave, West Palm Beach, FL 33408	1,2	83	8,311	2.6	97.6	0.9	3.6	53,730	271	272
Sagrada Familia, 970 SW 1st St, Miami, FL 33131	2	26	7,613	2.1	93.3	1.7	54.6	56,297	275	293
Stephanis Unit (Boys and Girls Club), 212 NW 16th St, Pompano Beach, FL 33060	2	37	6,518	9.4	54.7	41.2	11.9	34,060	275	289
Teen Upward Bound, 490 Ali Baba Ave, Opa Locka, FL 33055	1	22	12,183	12.1	51.0	41.8	52.6	39,088	264	259
Village Academy (Beacon), 555 NW 4th Street, Delray Beach, FL 33444	3	36	6,050	10.8	42.7	54.0	9.4	36,335	325	323

Table 4.1—Continued

Site	Study Group	Children in Study	Crime Rate[a]	Single Mother (%)[b,c]	Race or Ethnicity (%)[b,d]			Median Income ($)[b]	3rd Grade FCAT Scores[e]	
					White	Black	Latino		Reading	Math
West Coast School, 10500 NW 7th Ave, Miami, FL 33150	1	15	7,613	16.3	18.3	78.5	18.6	21,775	288	307

[a] Crime rate is per 100,000 population from 2005 Florida Department of Law Enforcement data for local jurisdiction.

[b] Single-mother home, race and ethnicity, and median income pertain to ZIP code and are from 2000 census.

[c] Single-mother homes are female householder, no husband present, with own children under 18 years.

[d] Census race and ethnicity categories are not mutually exclusive.

[e] FCAT scores are mean 2006 Florida Comprehensive Assessment Test scores for nearest public school.

Figure 4.2
Map of Participating After-School–Program Sites in Miami-Dade Area, Florida

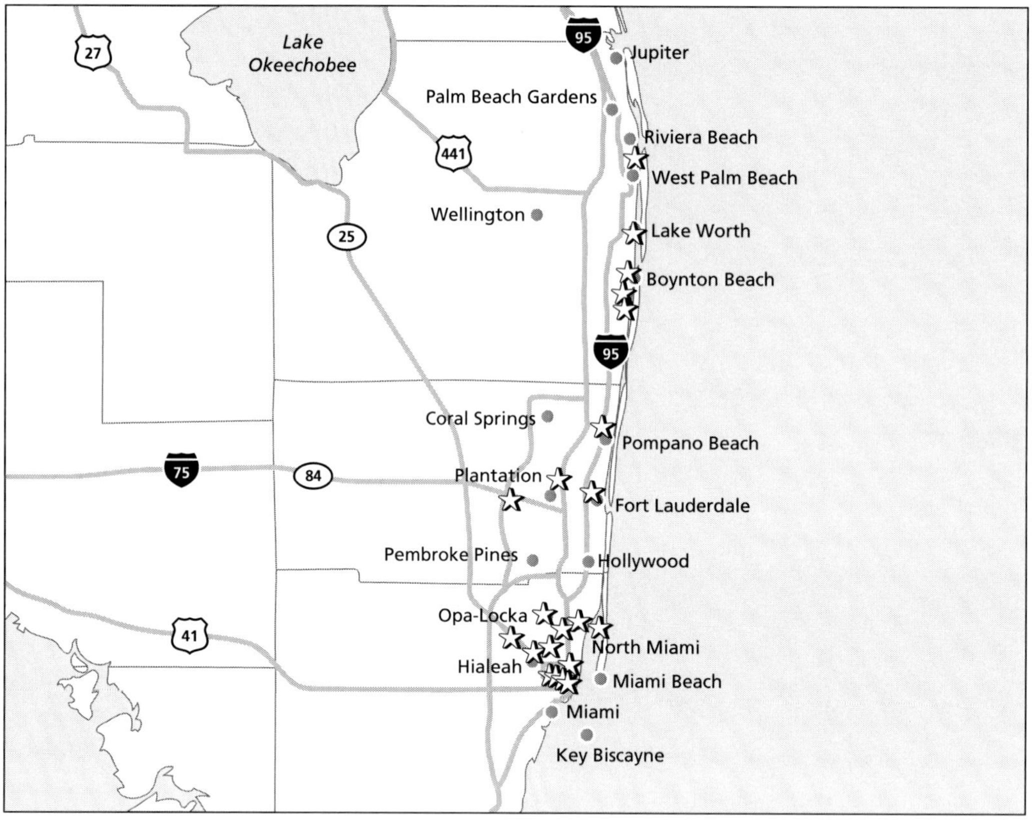

RAND *TR575-4.2*

as a control group, is retained in the treatment group. As we show next, this strategy produces fairly well-balanced treatment and control groups in the teacher data, but, even to the extent that a few site-level differences persist, they are easily controlled by the site-level fixed effects.

A final design note is that, since randomization occurred at the site level rather than the individual level and the sites are located in different communities, there is little risk of the control group being contaminated by diffusion or "spillover" effects (i.e., treatment-group children sharing what they were learning with control-group children). There may be positive treatment externalities extending to other non-SFK children in the site, but we did not have the resources to collect this kind of data.

Assessment Instrument: The Behavior Assessment System for Children, Second Edition

All measurements were taken using a common published instrument, the Behavior Assessment System for Children, Second Edition (BASC-2). The BASC-2 is a multimethod, multidimensional system used to evaluate the behavior and self-perceptions of children and young adults aged 2 through 25 years. It consists of two rating scales, one for teachers (teacher rating scales, or TRSs) and one for parents (parent rating scales, or PRSs), which collect data about the child's observable behavior, each divided into age-appropriate forms. It also includes a self-report scale (self-report of personality, or SRP), on which the child or young adult can describe his or her behaviors, emotions, and self-perceptions.

The BASC-2 measures numerous aspects of behavior and personality, including positive (adaptive) as well as negative (clinical) dimensions, and, importantly, behaviors that relate to the explicit program goals of SFK. The BASC-2 components may be used separately or in combination to provide information about a child from multiple sources. Certain scales are common across sources, permitting direct comparison of ratings from different sources on the same measure. An invaluable feature of the BASC-2 is that it has built-in validity checks to help detect misunderstanding, carelessness, or untruthful responding. The BASC-2 questionnaire also asks for age, sex, and grade of the child. Since its inception in 1985, the BASC-2 has been widely used in research as well as in clinical (i.e., school) settings.

Data Collection

Under RAND direction and oversight, the SFK research director coordinated data collection. The RAND principal investigator made one visit to SFK headquarters in Miami during November 2006 to inspect protocols for data collection, storage, management, and protection of confidentiality and to observe test administration at one randomly chosen program site.

Data were collected from children and teachers. The teachers in question were *not* the SFK program teachers but rather the regular after-school program teachers at the host sites and had no involvement in the teaching of the SFK classes. In most cases, pretesting of children took place on designated introduction days prior to implementation of the first lesson of the course; just 9 percent of children took their pretests after programming began. Children ages 8 to 11 were administered the BASC-2 SRP-child (SRP-C), and a small number of children ages 12 to 14 were administered the SRP-adolescent (SRP-A). Posttesting followed the last lesson of the class, and follow-up testing of treatment-group children occurred approximately 12 weeks thereafter.

Teachers did not undergo testing as a group; rather, they were instructed to complete the BASC-2 questionnaires for each of their children enrolled in the study prior to the beginning of the first lesson of the course and again shortly after the final lesson. Because of the response burden imposed on teachers, they were given a $25 Target® gift card after completion of each set of surveys. In actuality, 53 percent of teacher rating forms were completed shortly after programming began (usually after the first class but before the second class). Teachers completed the BASC-2 TRS (TRS-C or TRS-A, depending on the age of the subject child). All BASC-2 questionnaires were in English (as was the SFK programming). All item responses were entered by hand into the BASC-2 ASSIST™ software, and every fourth record was double-checked. All scoring was computed by the BASC-2 ASSIST software.

An attempt was made to collect data from parents, but a small pilot study conducted in early 2006 revealed this to be extraordinarily difficult, since the parents were rarely present at the program sites. Attempts to mail questionnaires or send parent questionnaires home with children were fruitless. Instead, we re-allocated resources to securing parental consent for the children to participate in the study.[3] This was accomplished by holding special training sessions

---

[3]   Children were also required to sign assent forms to participate in the study. Although parental consent and child assent were not required for a student to take the SFK course, both were required for participation in this study. Consent was also

at each of the sites to organize the regular (i.e., non-SFK) after-school–program staff to make focused efforts to connect with parents, inform them about the study, and obtain signed consent forms. These activities significantly boosted response rates. Although no formal data on response rates are available, we informally estimate that the response rate by parents regarding their child's participation in the study was approximately 95 percent. The total number of children enrolled in the study was 737. Of these, teachers completed questionnaires for 89 percent of children enrolled in the study, and 53 percent of children completed self-report questionnaires. Importantly, response rates were not affected by ability or willingness to pay for the SFK course. As noted previously, the SFK program is free to participating families, and, since SFK supplies the teaching staff, it requires no resources from the host site beyond space.

Randomization

Randomization was implemented over 19 sites, not children. Under the supervision of the RAND principal investigator, the SFK research director carried out randomization. There were a few departures from random assignment to accommodate the scheduling needs of some sites, but these were verified to have been for idiosyncratic reasons, entirely unrelated to the propensity of children in the site to benefit from the SFK curriculum.[4]

After randomization, non-SFK staff at each after-school program site recruited and enrolled children in the study. Typically, site program staff determined which groups of children would participate in the SFK course, then made extensive efforts to collect informed-consent forms from as many parents as possible.

As noted above, we pooled all treatment-group observations across the study waves and all control-group observations. In Tables 4.2 and 4.4, we assess whether the treatment and control groups were balanced in terms of observable characteristics. Table 4.2 presents results from a logistic regression of treatment-group status on baseline (pretest) characteristics of children in the sample of teacher reports. In terms of neighborhood characteristics, the treatment group was composed of children from neighborhoods with higher crime rates and with higher percentages of both whites and blacks compared to those of other racial or ethnic groups.[5] At the 10-percent significance level, there are also differences in percentages of single mothers and Latinos in the surrounding neighborhood. These differences point to a tendency for treatment-group children to come from relatively disadvantaged neighborhoods, which might create bias against finding program effects.

There are no statistically significant differences across the treatment and control groups in mean standardized-test scores at nearby schools (third- and tenth-grade reading and math), age of study children (measured at the individual level), gender of study children (also an

---

obtained from the teachers participating in the study. The RAND Institutional Review Board approved all consent forms and the research protocol for this study.

[4] Because SFK is a relatively short intervention, programming needed to be delivered on the same weekday throughout 12 consecutive weeks (10 weeks of classes plus one week each for pre- and posttesting). Therefore, scheduling had to work around previously scheduled activities, field trips, school closures, and holidays. In most cases, program staff were able to find at least one weekday that was consecutively free of interruption during the assigned study period. However, in a few instances, there was no alternative but to move a site to a different cycle of the study.

[5] Since we do not measure race or ethnicity at the individual level, we do not know whether these differences exist among the children in the study.

Table 4.2
Logistic Regression of Treatment Assignment on Baseline Characteristics: Teacher Reports

Baseline Characteristic	Coefficient	Standard Error[a]	p-value
Neighborhood demographics[b]			
Total crime rate per 100,000 people[c]	0.001	0.000	0.050**
Single-mother homes (%)	0.413	0.249	0.097*
White (%)	0.881	0.354	0.013**
Black (%)	0.787	0.308	0.010**
Latino (%)	0.034	0.019	0.080*
Median income ($1,000)	−0.090	0.056	0.107
Neighborhood test scores			
Third-grade reading FCAT score[d]	−0.005	0.039	0.887
Third-grade math FCAT score[d]	0.005	0.041	0.909
10th-grade reading FCAT score[d]	0.029	0.096	0.759
10th-grade math FCAT score[d]	−0.030	0.096	0.757
Child demographics			
Child age	0.021	0.071	0.768
Gender (female=1)	−0.058	0.138	0.676
Non-SFK programming at site			
Music, theater, arts (%)	0.361	1.592	0.821
Sports, dance (%)	1.211	1.005	0.228
Leadership, mentorship, self-esteem (%)	0.370	0.890	0.677
Academic enrichment (%)	−0.026	0.645	0.967
Baseline BASC-2 T-scores			
Adaptability	−0.015	0.024	0.536
Aggression	0.015	0.020	0.470
Anxiety	−0.016	0.016	0.323
Attention problems	−0.001	0.018	0.940
Atypicality	−0.001	0.012	0.919
Conduct problems	−0.018	0.013	0.174
Depression	−0.016	0.018	0.392
Functional communication	−0.009	0.028	0.757
Hyperactivity	0.010	0.019	0.578

Table 4.2—Continued

Baseline Characteristic	Coefficient	Standard Error[a]	p-value
Leadership	−0.003	0.019	0.868
Learning problems	−0.051	0.017	0.002**
Social skills	0.040	0.033	0.218
Somatization	0.008	0.015	0.569
Study skills	−0.032	0.024	0.184
Withdrawal	0.008	0.015	0.597

NOTE: * indicates statistical significance at the 10-percent level. ** indicates statistical significance at the 5-percent level. Estimation sample is all teacher observations at pretest less 21 observations with missing values on at least one BASC-2 scale. Composite scales are excluded from regression, since they are linear combinations of other scales. Reference group for other site programming includes sites with computer and free-time programming.

[a] Standard errors clustered by school.

[b] Other neighborhood demographics are from 2000 census by ZIP code.

[c] Crime rates are from 2005 Florida Department of Law Enforcement data by jurisdiction.

[d] FCAT scores are 2006 Florida Comprehensive Assessment test mean scores from nearest school.

Table 4.3
Joint Significance Tests for Table 4.2

Statistic	F-Statistic[a]	p-Value
Neighborhood demographics	1.44	0.271
Neighborhood test scores	0.05	0.995
Child demographics	0.09	0.911
Non-SFK programming at site	0.69	0.610
Baseline BASC-2 T-scores	48.29	0.001**

NOTE: N = 869. * indicates statistical significance at the 10-percent level. ** indicates statistical significance at the 5-percent level.

[a] F-statistic pertains to adjusted Wald test.

Table 4.4
Logistic Regression of Treatment Assignment on Baseline Characteristics: Child Reports

Baseline Characteristic	Coefficient	Standard Error[a]	p-Value
Neighborhood demographics			
Total crime rate per 100,000 people[b]	0.001	0.000	0.015**
Single-mother homes (%)	0.460	0.343	0.180
White (%)	0.814	0.271	0.003**
Black (%)	0.730	0.227	0.001**
Latino (%)	0.023	0.023	0.315
Median income ($1,000)	−0.068	0.046	0.137

Table 4.4—Continued

Baseline Characteristic	Coefficient	Standard Error[a]	p-Value
Neighborhood test scores[c]			
Third-grade reading FCAT score	−0.063	0.045	0.163
Third-grade math FCAT score	0.058	0.045	0.198
10th-grade reading FCAT score	0.032	0.085	0.703
10th-grade math FCAT score	−0.040	0.088	0.646
Child demographics			
Child age	0.201	0.086	0.020**
Gender (female=1)	0.181	0.094	0.055*
Non-SFK programming at site			
Music, theater, arts (%)	0.546	1.590	0.731
Sports, dance (%)	0.867	1.393	0.534
Leadership, mentorship, self-esteem (%)	0.064	1.311	0.961
Academic enrichment (%)	−1.205	0.903	0.182
Baseline BASC-2 T-scores			
Anxiety	−0.030	0.011	0.008**
Attention problems	0.000	0.011	0.998
Attitude to school	−0.001	0.014	0.965
Attitude to teachers	0.013	0.009	0.130
Atypicality	−0.001	0.012	0.907
Depression	−0.009	0.015	0.568
Hyperactivity	0.028	0.008	0.001**
Interpersonal relations	0.016	0.013	0.198
Locus of control	−0.009	0.014	0.523
Relations with parents	0.018	0.008	0.019**
Self-esteem	−0.026	0.006	0.000**
Self-reliance	−0.025	0.012	0.037**
Sense of inadequacy	−0.023	0.009	0.011**
Social stress	0.012	0.014	0.397

NOTE: * indicates statistical significance at the 10-percent level. ** indicates statistical significance at the 5-percent level. Estimation sample is all child self-report observations present at pretest less 20 observations with missing values on at least one BASC-2 scale. Composite scales excluded from regression because they are linear combinations of other scales. Reference group for other site programming includes sites with computer and free-time programming.

[a] Standard errors clustered by school. F-statistic pertains to adjusted Wald test.

[b] Crime rates are from 2005 Florida Department of Law Enforcement data by jurisdiction. Other neighborhood demographics are from 2000 census by ZIP code.

[c] FCAT scores are 2006 FCAT mean scores from nearest school.

Table 4.5
Joint Significance Tests for Table 4.4

Statistic	F-Statistic	p-Value
Neighborhood demographics	1.99	0.147
Neighborhood test scores	0.88	0.503
Child demographics	2.86	0.087*
Non-SFK programming at site	0.44	0.779
Baseline BASC-2 t-scores	804.20	0.000**

NOTE: N = 519. * indicates statistical significanec at the 10-percent level. ** indicates statistical significance at the 5-percent level.

individual-level measure), and the availability of other types of programming at the sites (e.g., music, theatre, and arts; sports; leadership; academic enrichment; computer and free-time activities). There are no statistically significant differences between the treatment and control groups on 14 of the 15 BASC-2 behavioral scales (the composite scales are excluded from the regression, as they are combinations of the others). Indeed, the groups differ only with respect to baseline learning problems (less prevalent in the treatment group). Although there are no significant differences across 14 of the 15 scales, we reject the hypothesis that their coefficients are jointly equal to zero.

A similar regression model is shown for the child self-report data in Table 4.4. It is important to note that self-report data were collected for only 54 percent of participating children; this raises the possibility of nonresponse bias, which may or may not differentially affect the treatment and control groups. If so, nonresponse bias could either exacerbate or offset any group differences due to imperfect randomization. Compared to the teacher sample in Table 4.2, Table 4.4 shows the same statistically significant differences between treatment and control children in local crime rates and in racial and ethnic composition. However, there is also a statistically significant age difference (treatment-group children are older) and a marginally significant gender difference (treatment-group children are more likely to be girls). However, when tested jointly, we cannot reject the hypothesis that either the neighborhood coefficients or the child demographics are jointly zero. There are no statistically significant differences with respect to standardized-test scores at nearby schools, the percentages of single mothers, Latinos, median income in the surrounding neighborhood, or the availability of other types of programming at the sites. There are however, statistically significant differences in six out of the 14 individual BASC-2 scales, and, for the group, we reject the hypothesis that their coefficients are jointly zero. Because there are additional treatment and control differences in the child data that are not in the teacher data, we interpret this as evidence of some differential nonresponse bias. Consequently, we have less confidence in the quality of the child self-report data than we have in the teacher data.

Attrition

In any intervention study, attrition of subjects between pretest and posttest is expected. Ideally, attrition is random—that is, subjects leave the study for reasons unrelated to the intervention itself. More problematic is nonrandom attrition, whereby those who leave the study are either more or less likely to have benefited from the program. Random attrition does not bias estimated TEs, whereas nonrandom attrition may lead to biased effects.

We employ three methods to assess the extent and nature of attrition in the study. The first is to compare attrition rates for the treatment and control groups; if the rates are not statistically different, then one may infer that the attrition process was probably similar in both groups. In other words, it is unlikely that attrition differentially affected the treatment and control groups (Cook and Campbell, 1979; Lee, 2002). A second method is to regress an indicator of treatment or control status on baseline covariates among the "nonattritors," i.e., the subgroup of observations that remains at the posttest (Cook and Campbell, 1979). This regression can be directly compared with results from the same specification estimated on the full sample present at the pretest, which we showed for the teacher and child samples in Tables 4.2 and 4.4. If regression coefficients across the pretest and posttest samples are similar, then one may be reasonably confident that attrition did not differentially affect the composition of the treatment and control groups. A third and related method is to regress each baseline outcome measure on main and interaction effects between an indicator for treatment status and an indicator for attrition. A significant interaction term signals that attrition had a differential impact on a given outcome depending on treatment or control status.

Results from the first test are shown in Table 4.6, which presents attrition rates for the study separately for the treatment and control groups and for the teacher and child samples. In the teacher sample, we see that, while attrition was notable, the attrition rate itself is not statistically different between the groups. The attrition rates were 22 percent in the treatment group and 19 percent in the control group (p-value on difference=0.180). From this simple test, we infer that attrition in the teacher sample was not likely to have differentially affected the treatment and control groups. In the child sample, attrition was higher in the treatment group (40 percent) than in the control group (26 percent) (p-value on difference=0.001), which suggests that attrition may have differentially affected the groups. The reason for the different attrition patterns between the child and teacher samples is that children had to be physically present on the day of the posttest to be counted as nonattritors; that is, children who completed the SFK course but happened to be absent on the day of the posttest were classified as attritors. Teachers, on the other hand, could still complete questionnaires about these children, since they were free to complete the questionnaires on their own schedule and did not need the children to be present to do so.

In both samples, attrition rates by follow-up are much higher (57 percent in the teacher sample and 66 percent in the child sample) and are calculated only for the treatment group. Follow-up testing of the control group was never possible, because all control-group subjects were offered the intervention.

Results of the second test are shown in Tables 4.7 and 4.9. Table 4.7 presents results from a logistic regression of treatment or control status on baseline covariates for all nonattritors in the teacher sample. The coefficients can be directly compared to those in Table 4.2, which are based on an identical specification but estimated over all observations present at the pretest (i.e., the attritors and nonattritors pooled). The patterns of coefficients in Tables 4.2 and 4.7 are quite similar, and indeed, for each covariate, its coefficients are not statistically different across the two samples. Similarly for the child sample, one can make the same comparison between Table 4.9 and Table 4.4. Interestingly, there are fewer statistically significant coefficients at

Table 4.6
Attrition Rates

Characteristic	Treatment	Control	p-value
Teacher data			
Pre-post	0.22	0.19	0.180
Pre–follow up	0.57	—	
Child data			
Pre-post	0.40	0.26	0.001**
Pre–follow up	0.66	—	

NOTES: p-value pertains to t-test of difference between treatment- and control-group attrition rates. Follow-up data were not collected for the control group. * indicates statistical significanec at the 10-percent level. ** indicates statistical significance at the 5-percent level.

Table 4.7
Logistic Regression of Treatment Assignment on Baseline Characteristics: Teacher Reports, Nonattritors Only

Characteristic	Coefficient	Standard Error[a]	p-Value
Neighborhood demographics			
Total crime rate per 100,000 people[b]	0.001	0.000	0.034**
Single-mother homes (%)	0.452	0.222	0.042**
White (%)	0.862	0.286	0.003**
Black (%)	0.760	0.251	0.002**
Latino (%)	0.022	0.016	0.180
Median income ($1,000)	−0.089	0.049	0.067*
Neighborhood test scores[c]			
Third-grade reading FCAT score	−0.008	0.040	0.833
Third-grade math FCAT score	0.009	0.041	0.816
10th-grade reading FCAT score	0.027	0.090	0.765
10th-grade math FCAT score	−0.033	0.093	0.719
Child demographics			
Child age	−0.038	0.074	0.612
Gender (female=1)	0.175	0.127	0.169
Non-SFK programming at site			
Music, theater, arts (%)	0.000	1.537	1.000
Sports, dance (%)	1.389	1.007	0.168
Leadership, mentorship, self-esteem (%)	−0.401	0.815	0.622
Academic enrichment (%)	−0.414	0.694	0.551

Table 4.7—Continued

Characteristic	Coefficient	Standard Error[a]	p-Value
Baseline BASC-2 t-scores			
Adaptability	−0.012	0.027	0.659
Aggression	0.014	0.019	0.465
Anxiety	−0.008	0.014	0.543
Attention problems	−0.003	0.017	0.853
Atypicality	−0.006	0.011	0.582
Conduct problems	−0.025	0.016	0.124
Depression	−0.018	0.019	0.334
Functional communication	0.000	0.027	0.995
Hyperactivity	0.016	0.023	0.472
Leadership	0.003	0.018	0.872
Learning problems	−0.049	0.018	0.006**
Social skills	0.026	0.033	0.436
Somatization	0.014	0.015	0.348
Study skills	−0.044	0.024	0.070*
Withdrawal	0.016	0.017	0.330

NOTES: * indicates statistical significance at the 10-percent level.** indicates statistical significance at the 5-percent level. Composite scales excluded from regression because they are linear combinations of other scales. Reference group for other site programming includes sites with computer and free-time programming.

[a] Standard errors clustered by site. Estimation sample is all nonattritors in teacher sample less 18 observations with missing values on at least one BASC-2 scale.

[b] Crime rates are from 2005 Florida Department of Law Enforcement data by jurisdiction. Other neighborhood demographics are from 2000 census by ZIP code.

[c] FCAT scores are 2006 FCAT mean scores from nearest school.

Table 4.8
Joint Significance Tests for Table 4.7

Statistic	F-Statistic	p-Value
Neighborhood demographics	1.94	0.149
Neighborhood test scores	0.07	0.990
Child demographics	0.90	0.427
Non-SFK programming at site	0.44	0.778
Baseline BASC-2 t-scores	166.14	0.000**

NOTE: N = 684. * indicates statistical significane at the 10-percent level. ** indicates statistical significance at the 5-percent level.

posttest (Table 4.9) than at pretest (Table 4.4); however, across the two tables, there are no statistically different coefficient pairs for any of the covariates.

Table 4.9
Logistic Regression of Treatment Assignment on Baseline Characteristics: Child Reports, Nonattritors Only

Characteristic	Coefficient	Standard Error[a]	p-Value
Neighborhood demographics			
Total crime rate per 100,000 people[b]	0.001	0.000	0.008**
Single-mother homes (%)	0.245	0.370	0.508
White (%)	0.672	0.250	0.007**
Black (%)	0.629	0.210	0.003**
Latino (%)	0.020	0.027	0.456
Median income ($1000)	−0.056	0.044	0.207
Neighborhood test scores[c]			
Third-grade reading FCAT score	−0.022	0.047	0.635
Third-grade math FCAT score	0.024	0.044	0.582
10th-grade reading FCAT score	−0.030	0.097	0.757
10th-grade math FCAT score	0.029	0.102	0.776
Child demographics			
Child age	0.298	0.145	0.039**
Gender (female=1)	0.569	0.258	0.027**
Non-SFK programming at site			
Music, theater, arts (%)	0.784	1.472	0.595
Sports, dance (%)	−0.288	1.345	0.831
Leadership, mentorship, self-esteem (%)	0.917	1.373	0.504
Academic enrichment (%)	−0.223	1.047	0.831
Baseline BASC-2 t-scores			
Anxiety	−0.010	0.018	0.601
Attention problems	0.012	0.014	0.375
Attitude to school	−0.009	0.016	0.557
Attitude to teachers	0.024	0.013	0.076*
Atypicality	0.011	0.020	0.570
Depression	−0.009	0.018	0.616
Hyperactivity	0.017	0.016	0.299
Interpersonal relations	0.011	0.010	0.297
Locus of control	−0.026	0.023	0.253
Relations with parents	0.028	0.006	0.000**
Self-esteem	−0.021	0.007	0.004**

Table 4.9—Continued

Characteristic	Coefficient	Standard Error[a]	p-Value
Self-reliance	−0.037	0.010	0.000**
Sense of inadequacy	−0.051	0.020	0.011**
Social stress	0.009	0.018	0.600

NOTE: * indicates statistical significance at the 10-percent level. ** indicates statistical significance at the 5-percent level. Composite scales excluded from regression because they are linear combinations of other scales. Reference group for other site programming includes sites with computer and free-time programming.

[a] Standard errors clustered by site. Estimation sample is all nonattritors in child self-report sample less 14 observations with missing values on at least one BASC-2 scale.

[b] Crime rates are from 2005 Florida Department of Law Enforcement data by jurisdiction. Other neighborhood demographics are from 2000 census by ZIP code.

[c] FCAT scores are 2006 FCAT mean scores from nearest school.

Table 4.10
Joint Significance Tests for Table 4.9

Statistic	$\chi 2$ Statistic	p-value
Neighborhood demographics	2.00	0.144
Neighborhood test scores	0.27	0.894
Child demographics	3.49	0.055*
Non-SFK programming at site	0.16	0.956
Baseline BASC-2 t-scores	46.46	0.001**

NOTE: N = 336. * indicates statistical significane at the 10-percent level. ** indicates statistical significance at the 5-percent level.

In the interest of brevity, we do not also show results from the third test, which involved regressing every outcome measure on main effects and an interaction term between attrition and treatment indicators. To summarize the results, in the teacher sample, the interaction term was not statistically different from zero on 18 of the 20 individual and composite scales (exceptions being withdrawal and anxiety, both of which were lower at baseline for treatment-group attritors than for control-group attritors at baseline). In the child sample, the interaction term was not statistically different from zero for 17 out of 19 individual and composite scales (the exceptions being locus of control and social stress, both of which were higher at baseline among treatment-group attritors than among control-group attritors at baseline).

On balance, we conclude that there is little evidence of differential attrition in the teacher sample between pre- and posttest and mild evidence of differential attrition in the child sample between pre- and posttest. This is consistent with anecdotal evidence collected about the attrition process. Program staff informed us that a typical situation was one in which a child left the Boys and Girls Club, for example, not SFK per se.

A final note is warranted regarding attrition and our use of the follow-up data to estimate the persistence of TEs. As Table 4.6 shows, the attrition rate in the treatment group climbed dramatically between posttest and follow-up. Since we will compare pre- and follow-up–test differences for the treatment group with pre and posttest differences for the control group (there was no follow-up test for the control group), the very different attrition rates for the two groups under comparison indicates that very different attrition processes were likely at play. To verify this, we performed the same analyses in Tables 4.7 and 4.9 of regressing treatment status on baseline covariates among those present at follow-up (if in the treatment group) or posttest (if in the control group). These regressions revealed no differences in baseline behavioral scores but very significant differences in neighborhood demographic characteristics, as well as in the availability of alternative programming. While we can account for these site-level differences with site-level fixed effects, the follow-up results should be interpreted as only suggestive, since the underlying experimental variation is flawed.

Program Dosage

Related to attrition is the concept of program dosage. *Program dosage* refers to the amount of programming actually received by each participating child, or the "strength" of the treatment. For example, if the average child attended only two out of the ten classes, then one would perhaps question whether the program dosage was strong enough to justify any reported TEs. Weak program dosage can also be an explanation for lack of TEs. Children who attrited from the study naturally received a weaker program dosage, but it is also possible that nonattritors missed classes throughout the course. Since the SFK curriculum is developmental (i.e., progressive in nature), with each of the key concepts and activities building on each other throughout the 10-week program, it is important that children attend a significant majority of the classes. Upon consulting with an outside expert, we established an a priori threshold of seven out of 10 sessions to justify TEs.

To examine this further, Figure 4.3 shows the percentage of children attending each of the 10 classes.[6] Not surprisingly, attendance was highest in the first class, at 87 percent. As the course progressed, the attendance rate declined steadily to about 70 percent by class 6, where it remained thereafter. The average number of classes attended was 7.21, or 76 percent of all classes. The latter figure, expressed in percentage terms, accounts for the fact that about half of the sites offered the SFK curriculum in nine classes while the other half offered it in 10 classes.[7] Table 4.11 shows average child attendance by site along with the total number of classes offered. Attendance varied across the sites, from a low of about two-thirds of program attended (ASPIRA, Milagro Center, and Nan Knox Unit of the Boys and Girls Clubs of Broward County) to a high of 90 percent of classes attended (African Cultural Center). Overall, we conclude that program dosage was reasonable and exceeded the minimum a priori threshold; however, the variation in attendance rates across sites underscores the importance of controlling for site-specific factors when estimating TEs.

---

[6]   Attendance data are missing for 20 percent of children who received the intervention.

[7]   The curriculum is designed so that classes 9 and 10 may be delivered separately or combined in one class. The nine-class format was used when necessary to accommodate holiday breaks and other scheduling needs of the host sites.

**Figure 4.3
Attendance, by Class Number**

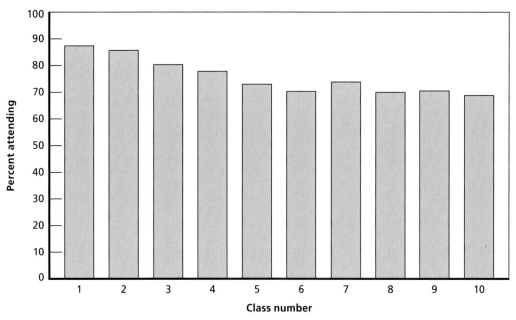

RAND TR575-4.3

Table 4.11
Attendance, by Site

Site	Average Number of Classes Attended	Number of Classes Offered
African Heritage Cultural Arts Center	9.0	10
Aspira	5.4	9
Centro Mater East	6.6	9 or 10
Centro Mater West	8.1	10
Citrus Grove Elementary (YWCA)	6.9	9
Concerned African Women	6.9	10
DeGeorge Unit (Boys and Girls Clubs)	6.8	9
For the Children	7.4	10
Forest Park Elementary (Beacon)	6.5	9
Hialeah Elementary (YMCA)	8.4	10
Lauderhill Unit (Boys and Girls Clubs)	6.4	9
Milagro Center	5.9	9
Nan Knox Unit (Boys and Girls Clubs)	5.6	9
Pleasant City	7.9	9 or 10
Sagrada Familia	8.4	10
Stephanis Unit (Boys and Girls Clubs)	7.0	9
Teen Upward Bound	8.0	9
Village Academy (Beacon)	7.4	9
West Coast School	8.7	10

NOTES: In sites offering only nine classes, content from classes 9 and 10 was combined in class 9. Attendance data are missing for 20 percent of children who received the intervention.

CHAPTER FIVE

Data Quality

Before turning to the outcome analysis, we undertake an examination of data quality. This is particularly important in the context of primary data collection and is essential for understanding how much weight should be placed on the results presented in Chapter Six. We use two methods to assess data quality. The first uses Cronbach's alpha to assess the reliability or internal consistency of each measurement scale, and the second uses indexes formed of special items embedded in the BASC-2 questionnaire that are designed to flag invalid response patterns.

Reliability

Because the BASC-2 is a published instrument, reliability has been extensively analyzed in a national sample of children. However, as noted by the Joint Committee on Standards for Educational Evaluation (1994), it is not sufficient to rely simply on the published reliability data without assessing reliability in our particular setting. Indeed, reliability measures may differ across settings owing to any number of differences in the characteristics of the children under study or in administration of the survey. When reliability is relatively low, results should be viewed with caution, as this indicates the presence of a large amount of random error relative to the amount of true information.

The first and third columns of Table 5.1 show Cronbach's α reliability coefficients for our sample separately for the teacher and child reports. The national reliability coefficients published in the BASC-2 manual are shown in the second and fourth columns for ease of comparison. For the SFK teacher reports, the reliability coefficients for most scales are similar to the national estimates, though almost always a few points lower. All scales are within acceptable limits, ranging from 0.76 (adaptability) to 0.96 (adaptive skills, behavioral symptoms index, externalizing problems). Reliability is higher for the composite scales, which is to be expected because they are composed of a greater number of items. The pattern is similar for the SFK child self-reports. The reliability coefficients are a few points lower for the SFK sample than for the national sample, and all but two scales (relations with parents and self-reliance) have reliability coefficients of 0.70 or higher. Contrasting the SFK teacher reports with the child reports, it is important to note that reliability is generally lower for the child reports than for the teacher reports. This is not unique to the SFK sample, as the same pattern is evident in the national samples as well. This implies that the teacher data are of higher quality, consisting of less random error.

Table 5.1
Data Quality: Cronbach's Alpha Reliability Coefficients

Characteristic	Teacher Reports TRS-C[a]		Child Self-Reports SRP-C	
	SFK Sample	National Sample	SFK Sample	National Sample
BASC-2 scales				
Adaptability	0.76	0.87	—	—
Aggression	0.91	0.93	—	—
Anxiety	0.82	0.81	0.81	0.86
Attention problems	0.87	0.95	0.70	0.76
Attitude to school	—	—	0.78	0.82
Attitude to teachers	—	—	0.75	0.72
Atypicality	0.88	0.84	0.79	0.84
Conduct problems	0.86	0.92	—	—
Depression	0.85	0.87	0.80	0.84
Functional communication	0.82	0.90	—	—
Hyperactivity	0.90	0.94	0.75	0.76
Interpersonal relations	—	—	0.81	0.81
Leadership	0.84	0.88	—	—
Learning problems	0.84	0.88	—	—
Locus of control	—	—	0.65	0.76
Relations with parents	—	—	0.79	0.81
Self-esteem	—	—	0.75	0.71
Self-reliance	—	—	0.61	0.71
Sense of inadequacy	—	—	0.70	0.78
Social skills	0.89	0.92	—	—
Social stress	—	—	0.77	0.81
Somatization	0.88	0.82	—	—
Study skills	0.87	0.91	—	—
Withdrawal	0.81	0.85	—	—
BASC-2 composite scales				
Adaptive skills	0.96	0.97	—	—
Behavioral symptoms index	0.96	0.97	—	—
Emotional symptoms index	—	—	0.92	0.94
Externalizing problems	0.96	0.97	—	—
Inattention/hyperactivity	—	—	0.84	0.85
Internalizing problems	0.94	0.90	0.94	0.96

Table 5.1—Continued

Characteristic	Teacher Reports TRS-C[a]		Child Self-Reports SRP-C	
	SFK Sample	National Sample	SFK Sample	National Sample
Personal adjustment	—	—	0.86	0.88
School problems	0.90	0.94	0.84	0.85

NOTE: — indicates no scale available.

[a] Teacher reports are from BASC-2 (2004) TRS-C. Child self-reports are from BASC-2 (2004) SRP-C.

Validity

Another way of assessing data quality is to use validity checks built into the survey instrument. An advantage of the BASC-2 instrument is that it uses a variety of methods to aid in detection of invalid results. For example, to guard against positive or negative response sets, it mixes both positively and negatively worded items and varies the possible response options (e.g., true-false versus never, sometimes, often, almost always). In addition, it includes special items whose sole purpose is to aid in detection of invalid response patterns. Based on these items, the BASC-2 software generates indexes measuring the extent of implausibly negative or "fake bad" responses (F index); overly idealized or "fake good" responses (L index); nonsensical responses due to carelessness or lack of cooperation (V index); repeated, alternating, or cyclical response patterns (e.g., marking all items *true*) (response-pattern index); or giving differing responses to items that are usually answered similarly (consistency index).[1] The BASC-2 manual specifies caution ranges for each of the indexes, and, based on these definitions, we created a binary variable for each index for which a value of 1 indicates the presence of a response pattern warranting caution or extreme caution for a given respondent.

Table 5.2 shows the frequencies of each type of invalid response pattern at pretest, posttest, and follow-up separately for the treatment and control groups and for teacher and child reports. Among the teacher reports, 25 to 30 percent of treatment-group responses exhibit at least one of the patterns warranting caution at pretest, posttest or follow-up—most commonly, inconsistencies in reporting across similar items, followed by fake bad responses. The pattern is similar for control-group responses, in which 26 to 33 percent of responses exhibit at least one invalid pattern—again, most commonly, of the inconsistency type, followed by fake bad responses. There are more fake bad responses by teachers among the control observations than among treatment observations, suggesting the possibility that some teachers may have attempted to "help" the evaluation effort by exaggerating behavior problems among children in the control group. Fortunately, we can use these caution indicators to control for such behavior when estimating TEs. Among the child reports, fully 46 to 51 percent

---

[1] The F index is a count of the number of times a respondent answered *almost always* to a question about maladaptive behaviors plus the number of times that respondent answered *never* to a question about adaptive behaviors. The L index is a count of the number of times a respondent answered *true* or *almost always* to an unrealistically positive self-description plus the number of times that respondent answered *false* or *never* to a mildly self-critical statement endorsed by most people. The V index is a count of the number of nonsensical items endorsed by a respondent (e.g., "I sleep with my schoolbooks"). The index for response pattern is a count of the number of times an item response differs from the previous item response. The consistency index is the sum of the absolute value of score differences between item pairs that are highly correlated.

Table 5.2
Data Quality: Percent of Observations with Invalid Response Patterns

Characteristic	Treatment						Control					
	Any	Inconsistency (Consistency Index)[a]	Fake Bad (F Index)[b]	Fake Good (L Index)[c]	Pattern (Response Pattern Index)[d]	Nonsensical (V Index)[e]	Any	Inconsistency (Consistency Index)[a]	Fake Bad (F Index)[b]	Fake Good (L Index)[c]	Pattern (Response Pattern Index)[d]	Nonsensical (V Index)[e]
Teacher data												
Pre	27	19	13	—	5	—	33	27	20	—	15	—
Post	30	21	9	—	7	—	26	20	13	—	2	—
Follow-up	25	15	7	—	8	—	26	20	13	—	2	—
Child data												
Pre	51	30	17	8	6	22	54	32	16	12	5	16
Post	46	26	19	6	7	25	49	31	18	8	7	22
Follow-up	46	28	23	5	3	24	48	31	18	8	3	22

NOTE: The determination of caution flags was made by BASC-2 ASSIST (2004).

[a] Consistency Index indicates differing responses to items that are usually answered similarly.

[b] F Index indicates inordinately negative responses.

[c] L Index indicates socially desirable responses or those that present an overly idealistic view.

[d] Response-pattern index indicates repeated, alternating, or cyclical patterns to responses.

[e] V Index indicates nonsensical responses.

of treatment-group children gave invalid response patterns at pretest, posttest, or follow-up—comprised predominantly of inconsistent responses, followed by nonsensical responses and fake bad responses. There was little tendency toward providing fake good responses or patterned responses. The frequencies for children in the control group were similar.

On balance, we judge reliability and validity to be within acceptable ranges for the teacher reports but recommend inclusion of the validity indicators in regression models to control for spurious variation contributed by invalid response patterns. Because this approach constrains the TEs for the valid and invalid responses to be identical, it is also necessary to compute the TEs for the subsample of respondents with valid response patterns.

We are less optimistic about the usefulness of the child self-report data. Although we can also include validity indicators to control for spurious variation, fully one-half of the sample exhibits a response pattern warranting caution. Given the smaller sample size for the child self-reports, the number of remaining valid responses is too small for meaningful statistical inference. The high frequencies of inconsistent and nonsensical responses (as opposed to fake good or bad responses) suggest that the children may have had difficulty with the BASC-2 questionnaire. Our observation of posttest administration at one randomly chosen site revealed this to be true. Several children seemed to have difficulty understanding the questions, while others had difficulty staying focused on the questionnaire, which had 139 items. This suggests that primary weight should be placed on the teacher reports and little, if any, weight should be placed on the child self-report data.

CHAPTER SIX

Outcome Analysis

In this chapter, we describe our estimation methods and results. We estimate the following model separately for each outcome in our data. Let y_{ist} be an outcome for child i in site s at time $t = 1,2,3$ (respectively denoting pretest, posttest, and follow-up). To estimate pre- and post-TEs, we regress y_{ist} on main effects and an interaction between a treatment-group indicator T_{ist} and a posttest indicator $I(t = 2)$, a set of indicator variables for each site D_s (i.e., site-level fixed effects), and a vector of individual-level covariates X_{ist}, as shown in Equation 6.1:

$$y_{ist} = \left(T_{ist} \times I\left(t = 2\right)\right)\theta + T_{ist}\delta + I\left(t = 2\right)\gamma + D_s\lambda + X_{ist}\beta + \varepsilon_{ist}.$$

(6.1)

The parameter θ is a difference-in-difference (DD) estimator of the program TE at post-test. The site indicators absorb all observable and unobservable fixed differences across the sites, such as differences in average child characteristics, average family background, the surrounding neighborhood, the quality of education at nearby schools, non-SFK programming offered at the sites, and other site-specific factors, such as the quality of program implementation or test administration.[1] The site indicators are identified because 11 out of 19 sites were randomly selected to serve first as control sites, then again as treatment sites. Therefore, we are drawing on quasiexperimental variation—that which occurs within sites over treatment status and time—to help identify TEs. The vector X_{ist} includes the individual-level measures of child age, child gender, invalid response patterns, and season. TEs between pretest and follow-up are obtained using the same specification except that $t = 3$.

As noted earlier, we stack all treatment- and control-group observations. This means that respondents in group 1 contribute up to two observations (pretest and posttest) and respondents in groups 2 and 3 contribute as many as four observations (pre- and posttest observations while in the control group and again while in the treatment group). The data structure for follow-up analyses is slightly different; respondents in group 1 contribute up to two observations (pretest and follow-up); those in group 2 contribute up to four observations (pre- and posttest observations while in the control group and pretest and follow-up observations while in the treatment group); and, since no follow-up test was given to those in group 3, those in group 3 contribute up to two observations (pretest and posttest observations while in the control group). Reported sample sizes also reflect a small amount of item nonresponse on the BASC-2 scales.

Because randomization occurred at the level of site rather than individual, proper statistical inference requires that standard errors be clustered by site. This error structure assumes that the disturbance term ε_{ist} is independent and identically distributed (i.i.d.) across sites but

---

[1] By *fixed*, we mean factors that are unlikely to change during the course of the 10-week intervention.

potentially correlated within sites. This yields a degree of freedom for the t-statistic equal to the number of randomization units minus one (i.e., 18), rather than the much larger degrees of freedom (based on the number of individual observations) that would obtain in the absence of clustering. This raises the threshold for statistical significance substantially (e.g., the critical value for significance at the 5-percent level with 18 degrees of freedom is 2.10 as opposed to the standard 1.96 that obtains in large samples). Since sites were sampled multiple times, it would also be possible to cluster the standard errors on the basis of site and study wave. This would raise the degrees of freedom available for inference (to 41) and lower the threshold for statistical significance (critical value equal to 2.02). However, we take the more conservative approach of clustering only on the basis of site.

Teacher-Reported Data

The BASC-2 scales may be classified as two types: clinical scales (measuring negative outcomes) and adaptive scales (measuring positive outcomes). The individual scales are further grouped into five composite scales, which summarize related scales in a particular domain. Table 6.1 lists the scales on which teachers reported and provides brief definitions of their content.

In Table 6.2, we present estimated TEs for the full sample and for the subsample of teachers with valid response patterns. We show the TEs between pretest and posttest and between pretest and follow-up. As noted earlier, the TEs at follow-up should be viewed as only suggestive because of the possibility of attrition bias. The scales are measured as T-scores, which are linear transformations of the raw scale scores, standardized to have a mean of 50 and a standard deviation of 10. This facilitates comparisons of TEs across the different scales. The reported TEs should be interpreted as the adjusted difference in mean outcome differences for the treatment group and the control group. Therefore, on a clinical (negative) scale, a negative sign indicates a greater reduction in the negative outcome for the treatment group, whereas a positive sign indicates a greater reduction for the control group. On the other hand, on an adaptive (positive) scale, a positive sign means a greater gain for the treatment group, whereas a negative sign indicates a greater gain for the control group.

Because of the large number of outcomes analyzed, we first present an overview of the general pattern of TEs for the individual scales and reserve detailed discussion of the TEs and corresponding ESs for the composite scales, which are groupings of individual scales. This reduces the dimensionality of the discussion and allows us to summarize the effects in a smaller number of broadly defined domains.

Of the 10 (noncomposite) clinical scales (aggression, anxiety, attention problems, atypicality, conduct problems, depression, hyperactivity, learning problems, somatization, and withdrawal), we estimate that the SFK program caused statistically significant reductions in one scale (attention problems) at the 5-percent level. When we exclude observations with invalid response patterns (about 25 percent of the sample), the estimated TEs become larger in nearly all cases, and four of the ten clinical scales are statistically significant at the 5-percent level, while another four scales are significant at the 10-percent level. Notably, all five of the adaptive scales (adaptability, functional communication, leadership, social skills, and

Table 6.1
BASC-2 Scales: Teacher (TRS-C)

Scale	Definition
Individual scales	
Adaptability[a]	The ability to adapt readily to changes in the environment
Aggression[b]	The tendency to act in a hostile manner (either verbal or physical) that is threatening to others
Anxiety[b]	The tendency to be nervous, fearful, or worried about real or imagined problems
Attention problems[b]	The tendency to be easily distracted and unable to concentrate more than momentarily
Atypicality[b]	The tendency to behave in ways that are considered odd or commonly associated with psychosis
Conduct problems[b]	The tendency to engage in antisocial and rule-breaking behavior, including destroying property
Depression[b]	Feelings of unhappiness, sadness, and stress that may result in an inability to carry out everyday activities or may bring on thoughts of suicide
Functional communication[a]	The ability to express ideas and communicate in a way others can easily understand
Hyperactivity[b]	The tendency to be overly active, rush through work or activities, and act without thinking
Leadership[a]	The skills associated with accomplishing academic, social, or community goals, including the ability to work with others
Learning problems[b]	The presence of academic difficulties, particularly understanding or completing homework
Social skills[a]	The skills necessary for integrating successfully with peers and adults in home, school, and community settings
Somatization[b]	The tendency to be overly sensitive to and complain about relatively minor physical problems and discomforts
Study skills[a]	The skills that are conducive to strong academic performance, including organizational skills and good study habits
Withdrawal[b]	The tendency to evade others to avoid social contact
Composite scales	
Externalizing problems[b]	Combination of hyperactivity, aggression, and conduct scales
Internalizing problems[b]	Combination of anxiety, depression, and somatization scales
School problems[b]	Combination of learning problems and attention problems scales
Behavioral symptoms index[b]	Combination of hyperactivity, aggression depression, attention problems, atypicality, and withdrawal scales
Adaptive skills[a]	Combination of adaptability, social skills, leadership, study skills, and functional communication scales

SOURCE: BASC-2 Manual (2004).

[a] Adaptive (positive) scale.

[b] Clinical (negative) scale.

Table 6.2
Treatment Effects: Teacher Reports

BASC-2 Scale	TEs at Posttest				TEs at Follow-Up			
	All Observations		Valid Observations Only		All Observations		Valid Observations Only	
	TE	p-Value	TE	p-Value	TE	p-Value	TE	p-Value
Adaptability[a]	4.9	0.003**	5.9	0.006**	3.5	0.168	5.0	0.120
Adaptive skills[b]	5.4	0.002**	7.2	0.001**	3.9	0.172	6.2	0.084*
Aggression[c]	−2.1	0.236	−2.9	0.092*	−1.6	0.489	−1.9	0.338
Anxiety[c]	−1.5	0.555	−2.2	0.218	−4.1	0.113	−2.3	0.301
Attention problems[c]	−2.9	0.036**	−4.6	0.007**	−1.9	0.333	−3.9	0.085*
Atypicality[c]	−1.7	0.442	−3.9	0.028**	−7.2	0.004**	−7.4	0.001**
Behavioral symptoms index[d]	−2.3	0.159	−4.5	0.006**	−4.3	0.023**	−4.9	0.007**
Conduct problems[c]	−1.6	0.239	−3.0	0.074*	−1.2	0.512	−0.4	0.802
Depression[c]	−0.9	0.595	−2.1	0.060*	−4.6	0.010**	−4.0	0.048**
Externalizing Problems[d]	−1.9	0.220	−3.4	0.036**	−1.0	0.604	−1.4	0.419
Functional communication[a]	5.8	0.001**	7.4	0.000**	7.5	0.007**	8.1	0.006**
Hyperactivity[c]	−1.6	0.319	−3.8	0.008**	0.0	0.995	−1.7	0.440
Internalizing problems[d]	−2.7	0.317	−2.8	0.104	−6.8	0.014**	−3.9	0.097*
Leadership[a]	4.2	0.050**	6.1	0.022**	1.9	0.516	4.9	0.193
Learning problems[c]	−2.0	0.114	−2.7	0.063*	−2.4	0.251	−2.9	0.158
School problems[d]	−2.7	0.047**	−4.0	0.015**	−2.4	0.186	−3.8	0.048**
Social skills[a]	3.6	0.056*	5.5	0.014**	1.0	0.708	3.8	0.275
Somatization[c]	−4.2	0.106	−2.5	0.128	−7.6	0.015**	−2.9	0.149
Study skills[a]	5.1	0.003**	6.7	0.001**	3.1	0.231	5.1	0.096*
Withdrawal[c]	−2.1	0.235	−4.1	0.031**	−5.0	0.033**	−3.9	0.141
Observations	1,574		1,117		1,310		941	

NOTE: ** Significant at the 5-percent level. * Significant at the 10-percent level. Rows present the estimated TE and p-value for listed outcome across different samples or models as indicated by column headings. All models are based on Equation 6.1 and include controls for age, gender, site-indicator variables, season of test, use of adolescent rating scale, and indicators for inconsistent response patterns. Standard errors clustered by site.

[a] Adaptive scale.

[b] Adaptive composite scale.

[c] Clinical scale.

[d] Clinical composite scale.

study skills) show statistically significant treatment effects (four scales below the 5-percent level and one scale at 5.6-percent confidence), and the treatment effects are larger in the subsample of valid observations (all significant at the 5-percent level).

On the composite scales, the effect of the SFK program on adaptive skills (a summary of the scales measuring appropriate emotional expression and control; communication skills; and prosocial, organizational, and study skills) was 5.4 points in the model with all observations and 7.2 points in the model with valid observations only. These are both statistically significant effects and correspond to ESs of 0.55 and 0.73, which are in the medium to large range.[2] In particular, they are large relative to the average ESs calculated by Durlak and Weissberg (2007) in their meta-analysis of after-school–program evaluations. By 12-week follow-up, the treatment effects (ESs) declined to 3.9 (0.41) (not significant) and 6.2 (0.64) (significant at 10-percent level) in the two samples.

The behavioral symptoms index, a composite measure of the overall level of problem behavior, also showed a statistically significant decline, with TEs of −2.3 and −4.5 in the full sample and valid-observation subsamples, respectively, with the former not significant and the latter significant at the 5-percent level. Both effects increased (in absolute value) by 12-week follow-up to −4.3 and −4.9 (both significant at the 5-percent level). These correspond to ESs of 0.19 and 0.37 at posttest and 0.36 and 0.40 at follow-up, all in the small to medium range.

On the scale for externalizing problems, a composite of the scales measuring disruptive behavior problems, the TEs were −1.9 for the full sample (not significant) and −3.4 for the subsample of valid observations (significant). These correspond to ESs of 0.16 and 0.29. However, the effects dissipated by 12-week follow-up.

On the scale for internalizing problems, a composite of the scales measuring overly controlled behaviors, the TEs (ESs) at posttest were −2.7 (0.18) and −2.8 (0.19), respectively, in the full sample and valid-observation subsamples (neither significant), rising to −6.8 (0.45) (significant at 5 percent) and −3.9 (0.26) (significant at 10 percent) at follow-up.

On the scale for school problems (a composite of the scales measuring academic difficulties, including motivation, attention, learning, and cognition), the TEs (ESs) were −2.7 (0.32) (significant) and −4.0 (0.48) (significant), respectively, in the full sample and valid-observation subsample at posttest and declined slightly to −2.4 (0.29) (not significant) and −3.8 (0.44) (significant at 10 percent) at follow-up.

While the follow-up effects certainly suggest reasonable persistence of many program effects, they should be interpreted with caution, as we cannot rule out the possibility of non-random-attrition bias in the follow-up data. In addition, in most cases in which we do find persistence of an effect at follow-up, we cannot reject the hypothesis that the follow-up effects are statistically different from the effects at posttest.

As a robustness check, we also reestimated all models using inverse probability weights. The weights were constructed by performing logistic regression on an indicator for remaining in the sample at posttest (or at follow-up) on baseline characteristics. The weight is the inverse of the predicted probability of being in the sample at each wave. At baseline, all observations

---

[2]   Since our estimated TEs may be interpreted as (adjusted) differences in means, dividing by the pretest standard deviation of each scale gives an approximation to Cohen's d, a common measure of ES. By convention, a Cohen's d of 0.2 is indicative of a small ES, 0.5 a medium ES, and 0.8 a large ES. Note that convention has it that a positive sign is assigned to an ES whenever the treatment group did "better" than the control group, and a negative sign is used whenever the control group did "better." This means that, for clinical scales, when the treatment group did better than the control group, the TE will be negative while the effect size will be reported as positive (Lipsey and Wilson, 2000).

have a weight of 1; however, at posttest, nonattriting observations with a high attrition probability are upweighted relative to those with a low attrition probability. Separate weights were constructed for attrition in the teacher sample by posttest and by follow-up. In all models, the attrition-weighted TEs were only slightly different from the unweighted TEs, and in no cases were the differences statistically significant (results not shown). This suggests that the unweighted TEs at posttest and at follow-up are robust to attrition.

We also estimated TEs on gain scores, but the loss of sample in the balanced panel increased estimated standard errors such that we have insufficient statistical power; this is exacerbated by the higher critical values we use to assess statistical significance. The point estimates were not statistically different from the DD estimates presented here, although they tended to be a bit smaller in magnitude.

Child Self-Report Data

Although we doubt the validity of the child self-report data owing to the large number of invalid response patterns, lower reliability coefficients, and the potential for nonresponse bias, for the sake of completeness, we present estimated TEs and ESs for the child data as well. Table 6.3 lists the scales on which children reported and gives brief definitions of their content, and Table 6.4 presents estimated TEs for the child self-report data using the specification in Equation 6.1. Two things are immediately obvious. First, for the full sample at posttest, there is just one statistically significant TE at the 5-percent level and one statistically significant effect at the 10-percent level. Second, the effects all go in the "wrong" direction, implying detrimental program effects. However, once we exclude the observations with invalid response patterns, all of the detrimental TEs switch signs, becoming beneficial TEs with ESs in the small to medium range. TEs are statistically different from zero for the self-esteem scale and marginally statistically significant for locus of control and interpersonal relations.

Dropping the invalid observations has a dramatic influence on the TEs at follow-up. On the individual scales, three of the ten clinical scales show statistically significant TEs at the 10-percent level, and one is statistically significant at the 5-percent level. One of the four adaptive scales is significant at 10 percent. The ESs are in the medium to large range in almost all cases. For the composite scales, the estimated TE at follow-up (in the valid-observation subsample only) for the index of emotional symptoms (a composite of the scales for social stress, anxiety, depression, and sense of inadequacy scales) is −6.2, corresponding to a large but marginally statistically significant ES of 0.61. This represents a more than doubling of the (imprecisely estimated) TE at posttest. Similarly, on the composite of internalizing problems (which includes scales for atypicality, locus of control, social stress, anxiety, depression, and sense of inadequacy), the TE at posttest more than doubles to −6.9 by follow-up, corresponding to a very large (significant at 10 percent) ES of 0.70. The TEs and ESs for the composite for personal adjustment (including scales for relations with parents, interpersonal relations, self-esteem, and self-reliance), the composite for school problems (including scales for attitude to school and attitude to teachers), and the composite for inattention and hyperactivity are also substantially larger at follow-up.

Table 6.3
BASC-2 Scales: Child (SRP-C)

Scale	Definition
Individual scales	
Anxiety[a]	Feelings of nervousness, worry, and fear; the tendency to be overwhelmed by problems
Attention problems[a]	The tendency to report being easily distracted and unable to concentrate more than momentarily
Attitude to school[a]	Feelings of alienation, hostility, and dissatisfaction regarding school
Attitude to teachers[a]	Feelings of resentment and dislike of teachers; beliefs that teachers are unfair, uncaring, or overly demanding
Atypicality[a]	The tendency toward bizarre thoughts or other thoughts and behaviors considered odd
Depression[a]	Feelings of unhappiness, sadness, and dejection; a belief that nothing goes right
Hyperactivity[a]	The tendency to report being overly active, rushing through work or activities, and acting without thinking
Interpersonal relations[b]	The perception of having good social relationships and friendships with peers
Locus of control[a]	The belief that rewards and punishments are controlled by external events or people
Relations with parents[b]	A positive regard toward parents and a feeling of being esteemed by them
Self-esteem[b]	Feelings of self-esteem, self-respect, and self-acceptance
Self-reliance[b]	Confidence in one's ability to solve problems; a believe in one's personal dependability and decisiveness
Sense of inadequacy[a]	Perceptions of being unsuccessful in school, unable to achieve one's goals, and generally inadequate
Social stress[a]	Feelings of stress and tension in personal relationships; a feeling of being excluded from social activities
Composite scales	
School problems[a]	Combination of attitude to school and attitude to teachers scales
Internalizing problems[a]	Combination of atypicality, locus of control, social stress, anxiety, depression, and sense of inadequacy scales
Inattention/hyperactivity[a]	Combination of attention problems and hyperactivity scales
Emotional symptoms index[a]	Combination of social stress, anxiety, depression, sense of inadequacy, self-esteem, and self-reliance scales
Personal adjustment[b]	Combination of relations with parents, interpersonal relations, self-esteem, and self-reliance scales

SOURCE: BASC-2 Manual (2004).

[a] Clinical (negative) scale.

[b] Adaptive (positive) scale.

While it is possible that treatment effects would rise following the conclusion of the intervention, it is less plausible that they would more than double in the absence of supportive follow-up programming. In addition, such large effects at follow-up are not confirmed by the teacher data; although it is worth noting that, for the two composite scales assessed for both

Table 6.4
Treatment Effects: Child Self-Reports

BASC-2 Scale	TEs at Post-Test				TEs at Follow-Up			
	All Observations		Valid Obs. Only		All Observations		Valid Obs. Only	
	TE	p-Value	TE	p-Value	TE	p-Value	TE	p-Value
Anxiety[a]	2.1	0.275	–2.4	0.267	0.6	0.843	–5.9	0.218
Attention problems[a]	1.0	0.618	–2.7	0.231	–1.1	0.690	–6.3	0.213
Attitude to school[a]	0.5	0.772	–1.4	0.638	0.4	0.839	–2.0	0.337
Attitude to teachers[a]	–0.3	0.837	–1.4	0.640	–5.0	0.043**	–8.1	0.072*
Atypicality[a]	3.0	0.003**	–1.6	0.394	0.1	0.970	–6.3	0.025**
Depression[a]	1.8	0.324	–2.1	0.217	1.5	0.550	–4.1	0.224
Emotional symptoms index[b]	1.9	0.266	–2.6	0.127	0.1	0.967	–6.2	0.065*
Hyperactivity[a]	0.5	0.804	–1.5	0.441	–1.6	0.583	–4.4	0.343
Inattention/ hyperactivity[b]	0.8	0.702	–2.3	0.248	–1.5	0.616	–5.7	0.264
Internalizing problems[b]	2.4	0.168	–2.5	0.104	0.5	0.867	–6.9	0.088*
Interpersonal relations[c]	–2.3	0.179	3.3	0.058*	–1.9	0.463	5.5	0.097*
Locus of control[a]	–0.1	0.950	–4.5	0.053*	–2.4	0.420	–8.3	0.077*
Personal adjustment[d]	–1.0	0.469	2.9	0.216	0.4	0.806	4.7	0.067*
Relations with parents[c]	–0.8	0.652	1.0	0.743	–0.7	0.718	0.5	0.877
School problems[b]	0.2	0.894	–1.5	0.608	–2.4	0.179	–5.5	0.082*
Self-esteem[c]	0.4	0.841	3.5	0.035**	0.9	0.612	4.5	0.135
Self-reliance[c]	–0.2	0.901	1.1	0.677	3.2	0.235	3.7	0.214
Sense of inadequacy[a]	2.5	0.219	–2.1	0.218	1.5	0.574	–4.5	0.249
Social stress[a]	2.9	0.078*	–0.2	0.897	0.9	0.722	–6.0	0.057*
Observations	886		444		739		367	

NOTE: ** Significant at the 5-percent level. * Significant at the 10-percent level. Rows present the estimated treatment effect (TE) and p-value for listed outcome across different samples/models as indicated by column headings. All models based on equation (1) in text, and include controls for age, gender, site indicator variables, season of test, use of adolescent rating scale, and indicators for inconsistent response patterns. Standard errors clustered by site.

[a] Clinical scale.

[b] Clinical composite scale.

[c] Adaptive scale.

[d] Adaptive composite scale.

the teachers and children (internalizing problems and school problems), there is significant growth between post-test and follow-up. Nonetheless, as we noted earlier, we cannot rule out the possibility of nonrandom attrition bias in the follow-up data; however, when we reestimate the follow-up effects applying inverse probability weights to adjust for attrition, the estimates change very little and are not significantly different from the unweighted estimates. Thus, the large follow-up effects may be generated not by attrition bias but by selection on the propensity to give a valid answer in the child follow-up sample. However, low statistical precision means that, in most cases, we cannot reject the hypothesis that the follow-up effects are statistically different from the effects at posttest.

Reconciling Results Across Multiple Informants

It is typically a challenge to reconcile results collected from multiple informants—in our case, the data collected from teachers and the data collected from the children themselves. Multiple informants can provide a more comprehensive picture of a child's behavior (Offord et al., 1996), but they frequently provide conflicting data in psychological research (Grills and Ollendick, 2003; Kraemer et al., 2003). For example, a meta-analysis of cross-informant reports of behavioral and emotional problems found that the average correlation between children's and teachers' reports was 0.20. Such low cross-informant correlations have been construed as casting doubt on one or both informants, but low correlations may instead indicate context (Achenbach, McConaughy, and Howell, 1987), different perspectives of the informants, or measurement error (Kraemer et al., 2003). Concordance may also vary by type of behavior (e.g., less concordance for internalizing disorders, greater concordance for externalizing disorders), gender, age, and social desirability (Grills and Ollendick, 2003). It is clear that each type of informant can provide unique data (Achenbach, McConaughy, and Howells, 1987; Offord et al., 1996), and none is a priori "better" than another (Grills and Ollendick, 2003). On the BASC-2, for example, only the child self-report instrument measures self-perceptions and attitudes. And despite its lower reliability than the teacher report, the child self-report provides data on positive attributes, unlike most other self-report measures (Burns, 2002). Nonetheless, Grills and Ollendick (2003) have suggested that children younger than 10 may not have the ability to describe their feelings and behaviors accurately. As children age, they may become better informants (Kraemer et al., 2003) and their self-reports may become more reliable (Fallon and Schwab-Stone, 1994).

There is little consensus about how to reconcile data from multiple informants. For the BASC-2 scales that are common to both teachers and children, we computed cross-informant correlations at pretest for the child subjects ages 8–11. These ranged from lows of 0.06 (anxiety) and 0.09 (depression), to highs of 0.21 (attention problems) and 0.22 (hyperactivity). Not surprisingly, the low correlations pertain to internal problems that may be more difficult for a teacher to detect, whereas the higher correlations pertain to external behavioral problems, which would be more readily observable by teachers. We found a similar pattern for child subjects ages 12–14.

Our overall assessment of the two data sources collected in this evaluation is that the teacher data should be given the most weight and the self-report data from the children be given less weight. The child data are plagued with invalid response patterns, which, in many cases, lead to perverse results. Observation of child testing by RAND researchers in one randomly chosen site indicated that some children had difficulty with the BASC-2 questionnaire. When we restrict our analyses to only those child responses with valid response patterns, we must necessarily drop half the sample, which calls into question external validity. The pattern among the remaining observations, while not entirely inconsistent with the results we found in the teacher data, consists of TEs arising between posttest and follow-up (as opposed to pretest and posttest) that are implausibly large, given the absence of supportive follow-up programming, and most likely a result of differential attrition bias by follow-up.

CHAPTER SEVEN

Conclusions and Recommendations

Based on the evidence presented here, we conclude that the SFK level 1 course had significant positive effects on the children in our study. The program positively affected virtually every domain covered by the BASC-2 assessment instrument, with ESs that ranged from small to large. While the program affected both clinical and adaptive behaviors, it had especially large effects on adaptive behaviors. This suggests that the program is an effective tool for both primary and secondary prevention.

In analyses not presented, we also examined whether effects for the treatment group varied with particular SFK teachers, controlling for site indicators and child characteristics. We found that, while attendance rates varied significantly by teacher, effects for the treatment group did not. This suggests that the program is delivered fairly uniformly by the SFK teachers and that the program's focused efforts on teacher training, as well as recruitment of professional teachers, has been sufficient to guarantee a minimum level of teacher quality.

While the effects for the treatment group did not vary significantly by SFK teacher, they did vary significantly across sites (holding SFK teacher constant) for some outcomes. While this could reflect any number of factors, among them is the possibility that TEs are sensitive to either the program setting or the characteristics of participating children. Because the program continues to expand to not only new communities but different countries and settings, we recommend a follow-up study to test replicability or generalizability of the SFK model across diverse contexts and target populations. For example, in southeast Florida, the program is delivered in school and after-school settings, in other countries, notably Mexico, Panama, and Malawi, it is delivered in family centers and orphanages. In addition, it would be worthwhile to evaluate the Spanish translation of the curriculum as delivered in the United States and Latin America to test whether TEs are robust to language differences.

While many program effects were reasonably persistent at 12-week follow-up, we noted some variation across outcomes in whether TEs rose or fell with time. This suggests that follow-up programming could be used to support the TEs achieved with the level 1 course. We note that, in some locations level 2 and level 3 courses are currently offered. We recommend evaluation of these courses as well to test whether they can support and perhaps even build on the TEs achieved after the level 1 course. In addition, we note that 12 weeks is a relatively short period for a follow-up evaluation; future evaluations might seek to extend the follow-up period. Finally, SFK's success in reducing the incidence of reported school problems suggests that an extremely interesting follow-up study would be to examine TEs on grades and subsequent standardized-test scores.

In documenting the first causal relationship between spiritual-development programming and behavioral outcomes, our analysis suggests that the SFK model is a powerful approach to creating positive outcomes for children. Although SFK is a noncognitive intervention, non-cognitive abilities (such as locus of control and self-esteem) have been found in other studies to positively influence future schooling decisions, labor-market productivity and wages, such behaviors as cigarette and marijuana use, the probability of incarceration (for men), and participation in crime; these effects are often much stronger than the effects of cognitive abilities (Heckman, Stixrud, and Urzua, 2006).

Training of Teachers and Facilitators

Prior to teaching, all new SFK teachers must undergo a three-month formal SFK teacher-training program. During the program, new teachers receive formal training by a local lead teacher, which includes an overview of the course's mission and goals, its key concepts and theory, and lesson-by-lesson instruction of all activities, games, and pedagogical techniques. New SFK teachers are asked to prepare and deliver key lessons for a group of their peers and the lead teacher for constructive review and feedback.

New teachers are not immediately assigned to their own classes. Instead, they serve as facilitators for the local lead teacher, gradually taking on more and more of the classroom delivery. Once a new teacher has his or her own class, the lead teacher holds regular meetings with each one to go over upcoming lessons and issues in the classroom, and identify additional training needs.

SFK facilitators receive a three-hour training course that includes an overview of the course's mission and goals, the key concepts of the program, a brief lesson-by-lesson overview of the content and major activities, and a child-abuse–prevention video. The training includes demonstration of selected activities from the curriculum and exercises in which an experienced facilitator leads a team of new facilitators through an activity as he or she would in the classroom. The goal of this training method is to help facilitators work through situations and questions that might arise in the classroom and teach them to consistently apply SFK language and tools. Weekly meetings of the entire teaching team are used to further practice upcoming lessons, discuss the intent of lesson activities, assign facilitator responsibilities in the upcoming class, and identify new training needs.

References

Achenbach, Thomas M., Stephanie H. McConaughy, and Catherine T. Howell, "Child/Adolescent Behavioral and Emotional Problems: Implications of Cross-Informant Correlations for Situational Specificity," *Psychological Bulletin*, Vol. 101, No. 2, March 1987, pp. 213–232.

Baker, D., and P. A. Witt, "Evaluation of the Impact of Two After-School Recreation Programs," *Journal of Park and Recreation Administration*, Vol. 14, No. 3, 1996, pp. 23–44.

Belgrave, Faye Z., Gretchen Chase-Vaughn, Famebridge Gray, Jerveada Dixon Addison, and Valerie R. Cherry, "The Effectiveness of a Culture and Gender-Specific Intervention for Increasing Resiliency Among African American Preadolescent Females," *Journal of Black Psychology*, Vol. 26, May 2000, pp. 133–147.

Benard, Bonnie, *Resiliency: What We Have Learned*, San Francisco, Calif.: WestEd, 2004.

Bodilly, Susan J., and Megan K. Beckett, *Making Out-of-School-Time Matter: Evidence for an Action Agenda*, Santa Monica, Calif.: RAND Corporation, MG-242-WF, 2005. As of April 8, 2008:
http://www.rand.org/pubs/monographs/MG242/

Brooks, Pauline E., Cynthia M. Mojica, and Robert E. Land, *Longitudinal Study of LA's Best After School Education and Enrichment Program, 1992–1994: Final Evaluation Report*, Los Angeles, Calif.: University of California, Graduate School of Education, Center for the Study of Evaluation, 1995.

Burns, Matthew K., "Self-Report Objective Measures of Personality for Children: A Review of Psychometric Properties for RQC," *Psychology in the Schools*, Vol. 39, No. 3, 2002, pp. 221–234.

Catalano, Richard F., M. Lisa Berglund, Jean A. M. Ryan, Heather S. Lonczak, and J. David Hawkins, "Positive Youth Development in the United States: Research Findings on Evaluations of Positive Youth Development Programs," *Annals of the American Academy of Political and Social Science*, Vol. 591, *Positive Development: Realizing the Potential of Youth*, January 2004, pp. 98–124.

Cook, Thomas D., and Donald Thomas Campbell, *Quasi-Experimentation: Design and Analysis Issues for Field Settings*, Boston, Mass.: Houghton Mifflin, 1979.

Donahue, Michael J., and Peter L. Benson, "Religion and the Well-Being of Adolescents," *Journal of Social Issues*, Vol. 51, No. 2, 1995, pp. 145–160.

Durlak, Joseph A., and Roger P. Weissberg, *The Impact of After-School Programs That Promote Personal and Social Skills*, Chicago, Ill.: Collaborative for Academic, Social, and Emotional Learning, 2007. As of April 8, 2008:
http://www.casel.org/downloads/ASP-Full.pdf

Fallon, Theodore Jr., and Mary Schwab-Stone, "Determinants of Reliability in Psychiatric Surveys of Children Aged 6–12," *Journal of Child Psychology and Psychiatry*, Vol. 35, No. 8, November 1994, pp. 1391–1408.

Fashola, Olatokunbo S., *Review of Extended-Day and After-School Programs and Their Effectiveness*, Baltimore, Md.: Center for Research on the Education of Students Placed at Risk, report 24, 1998.

Garza Fuentes, E., and J. E. LeCapitaine, "The Effects of a Primary Prevention Program on Hispanic Children," *Education*, Vol. 110, No. 3, 1990, pp. 298–303.

Gottfredson, Denise C., Stephanie A. Gerstenblith, David A. Soule, Shannon C. Womer, and Shaoli Lu, "Do After School Programs Reduce Delinquency? *Prevention Science*, Vol. 5, No. 4, December 2004, pp. 253–266.

Grills, Amie E., and Thomas H. Ollendick, "Multiple Informant Agreement and the Anxiety Disorders Interview Schedule for Parents and Children," *Journal of the American Academy of Child and Adolescent Psychiatry*, Vol. 42, No. 1, 2003, pp. 30–40.

Heckman, James J., Jora Stixrud, and Sergio Urzua, "The Effects of Cognitive and Noncognitive Abilities on Labor Market Outcomes and Social Behavior," *Journal of Labor Economics*, Vol. 24, No. 3, July 2006, pp. 411–482.

James-Burdumy, Susanne, Mark Dynarski, and John Deke, "When Elementary Schools Stay Open Late: Results from the National Evaluation of the 21st Century Community Learning Centers Program," *Educational Evaluation and Policy Analysis*, Vol. 29, No. 4, 2007, pp. 296–318.

Joint Committee on Standards for Educational Evaluation, *The Program Evaluation Standards: How to Assess Evaluations of Educational Programs*, 2nd ed., Thousand Oaks, Calif.: Sage Publications, 1994.

Kraemer, Helena C., Jeffrey R. Measelle, Jennifer C. Ablow, Marilyn J. Essex, W. Thomas Boyce, and David J. Kupfer, "A New Approach to Integrating Data from Multiple Informants in Psychiatric Assessment and Research: Mixing and Matching Contexts and Perspectives," *American Journal of Psychiatry*, Vol. 160, No. 9, 2003, pp. 1566–1577.

Lee, David Sang-Yoon, *Trimming for Bounds on Treatment Effects with Missing Outcomes*, Cambridge, Mass.: National Bureau of Economic Research technical working paper 277, 2002. As of April 8, 2008: http://papers.nber.org/papers/T0277.pdf

Lipsey, Mark W., and David Wilson, *Practical Meta-Analysis*, London: SAGE, 2000.

Little, Priscilla M. D., and Erin Harris, *Out-of-School Time Evaluation Snapshot*, Vol. 1: *A Review of Out-of-School Time Program Quasi-Experimental and Experimental Evaluation Results*, Cambridge, Mass.: Harvard Family Research Project, July 2003. As of April 8, 2008: http://www.gse.harvard.edu/hfrp/projects/afterschool/resources/snapshot1.html

LoSciuto, Leonard, Mark A. Freeman, Evan Harrington, Brian Altman, and Alden Lanphear, "An Outcome Evaluation of the Woodrock Youth Development Project," *Journal of Early Adolescence*, Vol. 17, February 1997, pp. 51–66.

LoSciuto, Leonard, Susan M. Hilbert, M. Margaretta Fox, Lorraine Porcellini, and Alden Lanphear, "A Two-Year Evaluation of the Wood Rock Youth Development Project," *Journal of Early Adolescence*, Vol. 19, November 1999, pp. 488–507.

Mason, Michael J., and Susan Chuang, "Culturally-Based After-School Arts Programming for Low-Income Urban Children: Adaptive and Preventive Effects," *Journal of Primary Prevention*, Vol. 22, No. 1, September 2001, pp. 45–54.

Miguel, Edward, and Michael Kremer, "Worms: Identifying Impacts on Education and Health in the Presence of Treatment Externalities," *Econometrica*, Vol. 72, No. 1, January 2004, pp. 159–217.

Offord, David R., Michael H. Boyle, Yvonne Racine, Peter Szatmari, Jan E. Fleming, Mark Sanford, and Ellen L. Lipman, "Integrating Assessment Data from Multiple Informants," *Journal of the American Academy of Child and Adolescent Psychiatry*, Vol. 35, No. 8, 1996, pp. 1078–1085.

Pierce, Lois H., and Nancy Shields, "The Be a Star Community-Based After-School Program: Developing Resiliency Factors in High-Risk Preadolescent Youth," *Journal of Community Psychology*, Vol. 26, No. 2, March 1998, pp. 175–183.

Scott-Little, Catherine, Mary Sue Hamann, and Stephen G. Jurs, "Evaluations of After-School Programs: A Meta-Evaluation of Methodologies and Narrative Synthesis of Findings," *American Journal of Evaluation*, Vol. 23, No. 4, Winter 2002, pp. 387–419.

Vandell, Deborah Lowe, Elizabeth R. Reisner, B. Bradford Brown, Kimberly Dadisman, Kim M. Pierce, Dale Lee, and Ellen M. Pechman, *The Study of Promising After-School Programs: Examination of Intermediate Outcomes in Year 2*, Madison, Wisc.: Wisconsin Center for Education Research, March 2005. As of April 10, 2008: http://www.wcer.wisc.edu/childcare/pdf/pp/year2_executive_summary_and_brief_report.pdf

Vandell, Deborah L., Elizabeth R. Reisner, Kim M. Pierce, B. Bradford Brown, Dale Lee, Daniel Bolt, and Ellen M. Pecham, *The Study of Promising After-School Programs: Examination of Longer Term Outcomes After Two Years of Program Experiences*, Madison, Wisc.: Wisconsin Center for Education Research, August 8, 2006. As of April 10, 2008:
http://www.wcer.wisc.edu/childcare/pdf/pp/year_3_report_final.pdf

Werner, Emmy E., and Ruth S. Smith, *Overcoming the Odds: High Risk Children from Birth to Adulthood*, Ithaca, N.Y.: Cornell University Press, 1992.